Poachers, Thugs a
A History of Crime
Bedfordshire

Table of Contents

Chapter One: Introduction

It is probably inevitable that when a local historian has finished a project and written up the results of their research that a new source of information is unearthed or, worse still, brought to their attention by a newly discovered relative of one of the characters mentioned in the recently published book. It was that inevitably that has driven me to tackle yet another project for Sharnbrook Local History Group (SLHG) within the general area of 'Law and Order'.

The first project focussed on the history of the Police Station/Court in the village and included an exhaustive study of the Parish Constable and Police Officers who served up until the station closed in 1967 when the Sharnbrook Division was absorbed into the Bedford 'B' Division and all staff operated from the Kempston Headquarters. That project culminated in 2012 with the publication of the book 'Beats, Boots and Thieves'. Its second chapter contained a rudimentary analysis of crime data and reported how crime levels were really quite low and mainly consisted of petty crimes. The comparison of crime levels with other villages in North Bedfordshire showed that Sharnbrook residents were on the whole rather law abiding. The most significant observation was how crime in our rural community differed from that seen in the urban areas and particularly with the levels of crime prevalent in the Luton Division. This difference has been consistent from the early C19th right through to 1967, the end date for the project.

The new data which became available related to some of the police officers who served towards the end of the study period. However it was the culmination of 'Paths to Crime' that was the most significant driver for the new project. 'Paths to Crime' was a 2 year project run at the Bedfordshire & Luton Archive (BLARS) and was led by Pamela Birch. The goal was to conserve

Poachers, Thugs and Thieves

A History of Crime in North Bedfordshire

Des Hoar

A publication of Sharnbrook Local History Group

Poachers, Thugs and Thieves
A History of Crime in North Bedfordshire

First published in 2016 by

Des Hoar

24 Loring Road

Sharnbrook

Bedford MK44 1JZ

ISBN 978-0-9574154-1-6

Front Cover: Impression of Victorian Poaching

Rear Cover: Cartoon of the theft of boots

Printed and bound in the UK by Biddles Books Limited.

the C19th Bedfordshire Quarter Session records and to fully index them to make them available through their online catalogue. The cataloguing, carried out by two part-time team members, was funded by a grant from the National Cataloguing Grant Programme for Archives. The repackaging was being carried out by volunteers and was made possible by generous donations from Bedfordshire Family History Society, present and former High Sheriffs of Bedfordshire and the Rotary Club of Sandy. The work involved reading every record and noting which people's names and place names should be indexed. The indexing also included details of both the offence and the outcome e.g. nature of any sentence. The ongoing results of this work were enticingly published as a regular feature entitled 'Crime of the Month' in the BLARS newsletter. This systematic approach to Quarter Session cases was inspirational in directing the new SLHG project to tackle a similar study of Petty Session cases held at the Bletsoe/Sharnbrook Division court. The goal would be to locate records relating to all Petty Session cases and to index them so the trends within the crime levels in North Bedfordshire could be studied.

Chapter Two: Methodology

Feasibility Study

A feasibility study clearly identified that there would be significant problems to overcome e.g.

- Incomplete records

- Unstructured records e.g. hand written notes in free text format with no tabular approach plus frequent use of undefined abbreviations

- Poorly written text which could not be easily read which would lead to either missing data or incorrect interpretations of the data.

It seemed that the level of clerical support given to Petty Session courts was somewhat less than seen in the Quarter Sessions and that the record keeping

 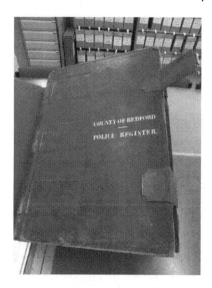

was less formal and certainly less structured. The problems might be surmountable if the court records could have been double –checked against police records but unfortunately there was no legal requirement to preserve this type of police record and only a fraction of the Sharnbrook Station's crime records remain available. The other source of ratification was the local newspaper. In the C19th the format of local newspapers was considerably more structured than seen today; it was quite normal for most of the Petty Session cases to be reported and a particularly interesting case may get the full treatment – what happened, witness reports, defendant's statement plus the outcome. Unfortunately not all cases got reported and there were occasional differences between what was recorded in the court records and what appeared in the newspaper.

The conclusion was that a systematic approach would be impossible

- for the first half of C19th because of the difficulties in reading and interpreting the data

- for the second half of the C19th because of the incompleteness of records.

There would be no value in indexing over 9000 cases if the analysis was unreliable.

It was concluded that the study should target only the years in which the annual national census was held. This would give annual datasets representing a slice of one year in every ten. The series of years would commence in 1841 which is very soon after the establishment of the Bedfordshire Constabulary and extend through to 1911, the latest date for data to be available under the 100 year rule controlling access to both detailed census returns and Police/Court records held at the County Archive. The study would ideally collect data from the relevant court record and then check whether more information is available through Police records, Gaol Records and newspapers. There was the added benefit that we may be able to better understand the social conditions of both the defendant and the plaintiff through the family data available in the census returns.

The data would be recorded on a case by case basis and data transcribed into a spreadsheet format with the following structure:

The DATE of the court meeting

The DATE of the offence

The PROSECUTOR'S (PLAINTIFF'S) NAME

The DEFENDANT'S NAME

The NATURE of the Offence

LOCATION of Offence

TYPE of offence (classification system)

Details of the JURISDICTION / OUTCOME

TYPE of OUTCOME (classification system)

NAMES of the Justices of Peace present in session

SOURCE of data

CROSS REFERENCE to QUARTER SESSION records

CROSS REFERENCE to BEDFORD GAOL records

Subsequently we added columns / conditional formatting to record

The NATURE of the prosecutor e.g. Victim, Victim's family, police officer, parish officer etc.

CROSS REFERENCE to any case was mentioned in LOCAL NEWSPAPERS

This database would allow us to analyze the crime records by year and across years. Where possible the overall crime levels would be compared to the independent annual inspection reports made by the Her Majesty's Inspectorate of Constabulary.

Synchronising the data from all three sources across a given calendar year would be difficult because court appearances in December may not result in gaol records until the following year. Reciprocally a gaol record in January might have come from a petty session judgement made the previous year. Also any cases requiring an adjournment would need special attention.

The Prevailing Court System

Throughout the study period 1841 – 1911 the court in Sharnbrook has been defined as a Petty Session i.e. the lowest tier of court within the national structure. This governs what type of cases can be heard within the court and thereby defines what cases have to be escalated to Quarter Sessions and /or the Assizes. It also defines the nature of the hearing i.e. it is under the total discretion of the magistrate(s) and without a jury. This is defined as Summary Jurisdiction.

Early on the court sessions for Bletsoe Division were mainly held at the Falcon Inn, Bletsoe although it did occasionally meet at other public houses in other villages in the Petty Session Division. Although the degree of formality at a Petty Session was substantially less than that seen at the Quarter Session in Bedford we can see that the consistent use of the Falcon Inn did reveal a continuity of authority since that venue had been used for formal meetings of the Hundreds for many years. This authority was partly based on the length of the term of appointment of a magistrate and the continuity of appointing magistrates from the small group of major landowners. It was also possible for the magistrate to hear a case at his own home and it was not unknown for the magistrate to furnish one of his rooms in his home to act specifically as a courtroom.

The court records were generally maintained by a court clerk who again was typically a long serving appointment. Several members of the Garrard family of Solicitors from Olney held the position in Bletsoe/Sharnbrook Division.

The particular magistrates who were serving at the beginning of the study period had been in that position for around 10 years. An Act of 1828 allowed quarter sessions to alter boundaries and to make new divisions. The establishment of the Petty Session was a reflection of the excessive workload being tackled by the Quarter Session, which, as its name suggests, only met 4 times per year. Petty Sessions were set up to deal with minor offences e.g. minor theft, assault, drunkenness, poaching, vagrancy, bastardy examinations etc.

Although it does not relate exactly to Bletsoe Division we are fortunate to have a Bedfordshire magistrate's diary relating to activities in his court prior to the 1828 Act. The magistrate is none other than Samuel Whitbread II who was the father of Samuel Charles Whitbread, the leader of the Quarter Session during the 1839 debate about the establishment of the County Police Force. His notebooks for 1810/11 and 1813/14 have been published and the originals are held at BLARS(1).

Approximately 80% of the earlier volume is in Whitbread's own handwriting. The second volume is entirely written by him. His court covered the villages and hamlets which became the Biggleswade Petty Session Division. The notebook was often written in a very detailed format and showed how he summoned witnesses to appear before him either on the same day or at 08:00 on the following day. Whitbread often had personal knowledge of either the plaintiff or the defendant and his reputation of justice tempered with honesty and kindness meant that people in Bedfordshire respected his attention to detail and overall fairness. The notebook shows that he does

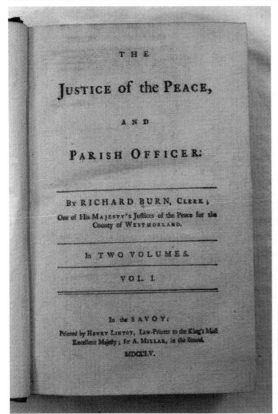

refer to a law reference book 'The Justice of the Peace and Parish Officer '(Richard Burn) 1755 and it shows that he also consulted with William Wilshire , another lawyer and magistrate who himself later became chairman of the Bedfordshire Quarter Session.

Samuel Whitbread was indeed a fine example of a 'patriarchal' magistrate. One can imagine that Lord St John of Bletsoe and Richard Orlebar of Hinwick were held in equal esteem within the Bletsoe Division. Samuel Whitbread had a strong interest in hunting and thereby a link to the Antonie family in Colworth. Together with the Duke of Bedford they had been responsible for the formation of the Oakley Hunt. Whitbread and Antonie had also been long term colleagues as Members of Parliament for Bedford.

Interestingly the notebooks do show a degree of firmness when it comes to Poaching. The evidence of witnesses is minutely recorded giving it a disproportionate significance. The local gentry were always eager to bring to justice the poachers who trespassed on their land. Commercial poaching, where gangs of poachers were going out at night to take large numbers of game, had increased during the latter part of the C18th and parliament's attitude had become stricter. An act in 1770 made imprisonment and public whipping the mandatory punishment. The Poaching Act allowed separate charges for hunting with dogs, possessing snares, setting snares, using a gun or using a net (for fish). Night poaching, particularly with a weapon, was regarded as a very serious offence and failure to pay the default fine was imprisonment for at least 3 months. Repeat offenders could expect imprisonment for up to one year and they could even be pressed in to the armed forces. The penalty for night poaching became even harsher after the end of the Napoleonic war when offenders convicted of armed night poaching were able to be sentenced to 7 years transportation.

In reality, only a small number of poachers were brought to court under the Night Poaching Acts. Most were charged under the old 'game code' with its default penalty of a fine or up to three months in prison. It was this level of activity that resulted in an appearance in front of the JP. A typical fine was £5 per offence and this could be multiplied up by the number of animals or the number of occurrences. It is not surprising that these prosecutions were often brought by the gamekeeper but they are also occasionally brought by a plaintiff who must be seen as a professional 'watcher,' a person paid to watch for illegal activity during the night.

Anyone caught and prosecuted for purchasing poached game was regarded with an equal degree of severity.

Defendants found guilty of Theft were also treated harshly. The only exception was where young boys were caught stealing apples from the orchards. Other thefts, including sheep stealing, were frequently escalated to the Quarter Session and maybe even to the assizes.

Assaults were common but the jurisdiction was surprisingly less severe e.g. payment of a surety to keep the peace. It was only if the fine was not paid that the prisoner had to wait in custody for an appearance at the next Quarter Session. It was also normal that the convicted offender had to pay costs e.g. for a doctor to attend the victim or for a constable's expenses.

Overall, the move from early C19th magistrate court to the 1828/9 Petty Session was only a marginal change. The responsibility for bringing a case before the magistrate was clearly still with the victim or the victim's family/representative. The Parish Constable's role was often to respond to an order from the magistrate to arrest a named individual and to bring them before the court to answer the case brought by the defendant. The cases brought before this lowest court were generally termed as misdemeanours. The magistrate had to decide whether the case should be escalated to the Quarter Session where the Grand Jury had to accept the charge as a 'true bill' and create the indictment which meant the defendant was required to appear before the next Quarter Session court. If the charge was rejected as 'ignoramus' the charge was dropped and the case was dismissed.

This reliance on the plaintiff to progress the charge and to provide a witness statement put a large strain on the whole system particularly if there was an existing family or business relationship between the plaintiff and the defendant. The magistrate was given a certain degree of freedom in handling and resolving each case e.g. if the victim asked the magistrate to act as a mediator or if they used a recognizance to ask the magistrate to bound over the defendant. It is generally thought that the magistrates, rather than escalate a case, would try to use their powers under whatever legal basis /authority they could muster to find a final resolution for a given case. In some instances this involved assigning an unusually low value to the stolen items so that a theft is classified as petty and hence can be handled summarily.

Samuel Whitbread had been in the ideal position to resolve many of the petty squabbles because he was the Parish Overseer of the Poor as well as the magistrate.

The magistrate also had the powers to allocate funds both to plaintiffs and to witnesses so their costs would be met and they therefore would not 'get a sudden bout of amnesia' and forget to attend the court session. You get the impression that Samuel Whitbread would not have tolerated any plaintiff or witness not turning up at 08:00 on the morning stipulated.

Using the data it will be possible to study the emerging role of the police force in acting as the plaintiff where they can be seen fulfilling a number of different relationships

- The person doing the detective work

- The person making the arrest

- The victim's representative

- The public prosecutor

As with Parish Constables, it was rare for a Police Constable to be an actual witness of a petty crime. The exception being an assault committed when the constable was trying to calm a riotous situation or resolve a domestic conflict. The Police may have taken over a prosecution where a victim was reluctant but having a reluctant witness would never help complete the prosecution.

The Police Officer would therefore, on occasion, have several roles

- The plaintiff bringing the charge

- The person conducting the case before the magistrate

- The witness to some aspect of the crime.

This multi-role scenario was more common in rural areas. The fact that a case was heard without the presence of members of the legal profession was of concern and the case of Webb vs Catchlove Dec 1886 appeared to rule in favour of involving the legal profession and therefore police advocacy was definitely discouraged. However not much changed and police officers continued to act as prosecutors in the lower courts.

The police possibly felt they had to act as plaintiff because of the frequent reluctance of the victim. This reluctance could have been due to

- They thought that the magistrate's attempt at mediation was sufficient and that no further action was needed

- They thought the defendants time in gaol prior to the court case was a sufficient punishment

- They thought the future relationship between them and the defendant would suffer if the defendant had a harsh conviction.

Although the summary court process was generally accessible to the majority of the population, it was highly discretionary. Individuals used the petty session for their own ends and the process was neither linear nor predictable in its outcome. The magistrate's role as a broker of settlement was as important as his role as judge of law.

The Samuel Whitbread notebooks were very much his personal records and contained a more personal and balanced view of the case compared to the brief systematic style seen within court records. When the defendant has both a family to support and a regular occupation, the jurisdiction was often more lenient whereas if the same crime was committed by a vagabond the penalty was usually more severe. Likewise, if the defendant was poor or of ill-health, the penalty was potentially reduced.

Summary jurisdiction has been conferred by individual statutes and bye-laws relating to a long list of petty offences. The most important perhaps are those under Acts relating to Game Laws, Highways, Public Health and Vagrancy. It does not include court sittings where either the magistrate is holding a preliminary inquiry as to an indictable offence or where the court is acting as the licensing authority. Within Bletsoe Division both of these two latter events do of course get recorded in the Petty Session minutes and are also regularly included in the local newspaper reports of the Petty Session.

Procedures at the summary trial of a petty offence were often very simple and expeditious. In the majority of cases there was no lawyer present for either the prosecution or the defence. If the defendant pleads guilty to the charge the court would often hear a concise report from the arresting officer and then a statement from the defendant. Further questions may be put to witnesses by the Clerk or the Magistrate. The defendant's criminal record is furnished, any additional character statements are heard and the sentence is then given by the magistrate. The process can be described as fast, simple and relatively cheap.

The practice of excluding lawyers for summary proceedings was outlawed in 1836. The Prisoner's Counsel Act gave defendants the right to be defended by counsel or attorney and to have witnesses cross-examined but still many cases went ahead without a lawyer.

Prior to 1847 the Petty courts would only hear non-indictable offences. In that year Parliament passed a law permitting children (<14year old) charged with theft to be heard summarily with the consent of the accused(2). Similiar conditions were applied to adults in 1855 for less serious types of larceny(3).

The 1879 Summary Jurisdiction Act (4) states that if the crime is liable for a term of imprisonment greater than 3 months and is not an Assault; the defendant may choose to have an indictment and a trial by jury. Should the court fail to give the defendant this information a conviction will be quashed even if the defendant had pleaded guilty. This applied even if the 3 month imprisonment only became applicable when the defendant's previous convictions became known to the magistrate.

At the end of our study period we see that wartime legislation greatly accelerated the move to allow magistrates to deal with new crimes without trial by jury e.g. trading with the enemy.

A county magistrate could, in theory, sit in any part of the county but in practice, tended to sit only in their locality. The splitting up of the Quarter Session began in 1828 and took a significant stride when in 1836 the Petty Session Divisions were created base approximately on the Poor Law Unions. Within North Bedfordshire the PSD took in most of the Stodden and Willey Hundreds but also included Milton Ernest because of its closeness to the Falcon Inn at Bletsoe. The early sessions were normally held at this large Public Inn on the main road leading north out of Bedford. The detailed nature of the newspaper reports suggests that these court sessions were not held behind closed doors.

The new PS Court was created in Sharnbrook as late as 1871; this was the last of the original 6 Bedfordshire Divisions to get a dedicated Police Station and Court. The building programme had been in response to the report by Her Majesty's Inspectorate of Constabulary and only just pre-empted the 1879 Act which attempted to discourage the use of hired rooms by limiting the powers of punishment. It was not until 1902 that using rooms in licensed premises became outlawed.

There were some examples to show that a sitting magistrate would step down for an individual case e.g. if the plaintiff was his own representative or if the defendant was an employee.

The 1879 Act also limited the maximum punishment which magistrates could impose by way of consecutive sentences to a period of 6 months. If the bench was not in a PSD court house the limit was further reduced to 2 months plus 20s fine. The 1879 Act also gave a general right of appeal to defendants sentenced to imprisonment without the option of paying a fine.

Across the country, the magistrates did not always of course have a good reputation. The magistrates, all male and drawn from the upper class, were thought to be prejudice against the lower classes and this was thought to manifest itself most in the harsh enforcement of the Game Laws where most defendants in cases of poaching were individuals from those lower orders.

For many years formal Petty Sessions were held at fortnightly intervals with normally 2 magistrates present. Informal sessions were also possible and could be heard at a magistrate's home. After arrest the accused may well have spent the time leading up to their appearance before the court in detention either at a Constable's home, or the Harrold lock-up or possibly in the Bedford Division cells.

If the defendant's crime was more serious and deemed a likely indictable case with its subsequent appearance at the next Quarter Session in Bedford, the defendant would normally have been committed in custody to Bedford Gaol. This could mean that the accused gets an entry in the gaol record even though he may have his case dismissed before or at the higher level court.

The style of the lower court was vastly different from the pomp and ceremony see at the Assizes Courts where the judges arrived in Bedford and were met with trumpets and javelin men before parading through the town to attend a service at St Paul's before the court was formally opened.

A study of the C19th national timeline of social history shows a period of political instability, so what was the nature of crime during the period?

In the early C19th, in Bedfordshire as a whole, we know that crime had been decreasing. The 1826 survey showed Bedfordshire as one of only 18 counties where the levels were down from the previous year. In fact Bedfordshire had the fourth largest fall in crime. The crime levels in north Bedfordshire villages were particularly low and the overall county crime level in the 1830s was almost totally dependent on the criminal activity in the Luton area. This difference in crime between urban and rural areas was the root of the difficulties in reaching an agreement on whether to raise extra taxes to pay for the county constabulary.

What were the crime levels in the county in 1830s?

Using the newly updated Quarter Session database (5) the number of records showed a moderate 22% increase from 703 in 1831 to 856 in 1840. A somewhat larger 44% increase is seen if you examine the records from the Bedford Gaol database (6)where the increase was from 164 to 237.

What patterns will we see when we examine the cases from the Petty Session Court?

References:

(1) Samue1 Whitbread Notebook

https://books.google.co.uk/books?id=LXavAwAAQBAJ&pg=PA25&lpg=PA25&dq=catchlove+1886&source=bl&ots=yM-on3bvZE&sig=BKuhOIWHE6vMXaZbhaBUz0wZK08&hl=en&sa=X&ved=0CCkQ6AEwA2oVChMlyrvx3MTTxwIVKyzbCh2RvAAC#v=onepage&q=catchlove%201886&f=false

(2) Juvenile Offenders Act 1847 10&11 Vict C.82

(3) Criminal Justice Act 1855 18&19 Vict . 126

(4) Summary Jurisdiction Act 1879 42&43 Vict C:49

(5) Paths to Crime Quarter Session database

http://bedsarchivescat.bedford.gov.uk/#Archive

(6) Bedford Gaol database http://apps.bedfordshire.gov.uk/grd/

Chapter Three: 1841

The previous decade had seen many significant political struggles across the nation. The 1832 Reform Act had finally given more people the right to vote since you now only had to own property or land valued at £10. The electorate was roughly doubled to 650,000 which was about 18% of the population. Although the reform of parliament had begun it still, of course, did not give the vote to the working classes or to women.

Life as a farm worker was dismal. A week's rent and basic food for a family would cost around 13s and the landowners were only paying as little as 7-9s per week. The Swing Riots had spread through much of the countryside and locally had included Stotfold and Flitwick. The Tolpuddle Martyrs were 6 men in Dorset who, in 1834, demanded 10s per week and wished to set up a fund for workers in need. They were arrested and transported to Australia. They became popular heroes and they were released in 1837.

The Chartist movement began in London in 1836 and sought further changes in the rights of the working class. In 1837 the novel Oliver Twist was published and it reflected a rather sarcastic comment on the Poor Laws.

A report of prisoner health at Bedford's new House of Correction in 1840 showed that land scurvy was a prevalent disease caused by the strict discipline of the prison, the scantiness of the diet and defects in the ventilation system. However, it also recorded that a prisoner suffering with varicose veins and two others with hernias did not have to work at the wheel even though they were sentenced to hard labour.

In 1836 the Royal Commission or Rural Policing had been established and their report in favour of creating a county-wide professional, full-time, paid police force was debated in the 1839 Bedford Quarter Session. For details of the differences between Samuel Whitbread and Earl de Grey on one side and Richard Orlebar and Lord St John, on the other side refer to 'Beat, Boots and Thieves' (1).

In 1840 the Bedfordshire Police Force was created and led by Chief Constable Capt Edward M Boultbee. Six superintendents and 40 officers were appointed across the 6 Petty Session Divisions. The first Superintendent for Bletsoe Division was William Whitmarsh and he immediately located his home and office in Sharnbrook. The other 6 officers in this Division were spread across the surrounding villages i.e. Riseley, Pavenham, Milton Ernest, Dean, Pertenhall and Poddington.

Robert Peel, Tory, started his second term of office as prime minister in 1841 and introduced a raft of legislation aimed at stabilising the economy and improving working conditions.

The first of the national censuses was held on the 6th June 1841 and Sharnbrook's registrar was John Williamson and the enumerator was James Coombs. The census return on 225 schedules showed 848 residents, an increase of 12% from an 1831 survey. The gender distribution was 414 males and 434 females; 279 (33%) were under the age of 14.

Sharnbrook was only the third most populated village in North Beds. The highest population was in Harrold and its greater commercial importance was clearly seen in the year's Pigot Directory .

The total population across all the villages covered by the Bletsoe Division was 14,343. At this time all the villages except Oakley had seen a population rise since 1831.

The Sharnbrook tradesmen two Bakers, two Blacksmiths, one bootmaker, three butchers, two millers, two tailors, a grocer, a carpenter, a lace dealer, a plumber, a stonemason, a watchmaker , a wheelwright and a surgeon. There were also two publicans, a vicar, a Baptist minister and a school master.

In addition the census showed 91 agricultural labourers, 20 skilled agricultural workers and 71 in domestic service.

What about the Petty Sessions?

During the entirety of 1841 the Petty Sessions were held by one or more of only 6 magistrates

Lord St John	WH Wade- Geary	RL Orlebar
Rev JB Magennis	Rev HD Ward	Rev V Alston

According to the Petty Session Minutes the most cases were heard by Wade-Geary (91) closely followed by St John (85). Ward was present for the fewest number of cases (48).

An image from the August records show the nature of the Court Register.

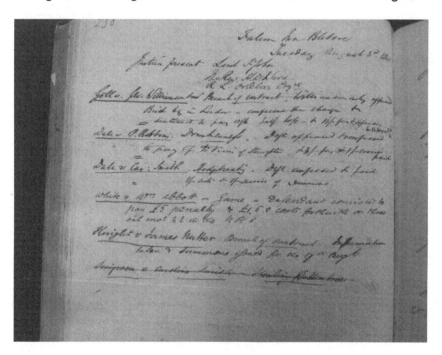

The Minutes were written in a non-structured format and the information was not always complete or consistent e.g. missing forenames or location. In one case even the nature of the crime was not recorded.

The cases were distributed across the year

Jan - Mar	Apr- Jun	Jul- Sep	Oct - Dec	Total
26	19	44	26	115

The highest number of case in any one session was 15.

So how many cases were heard in 1841 and what crimes were being dealt with?

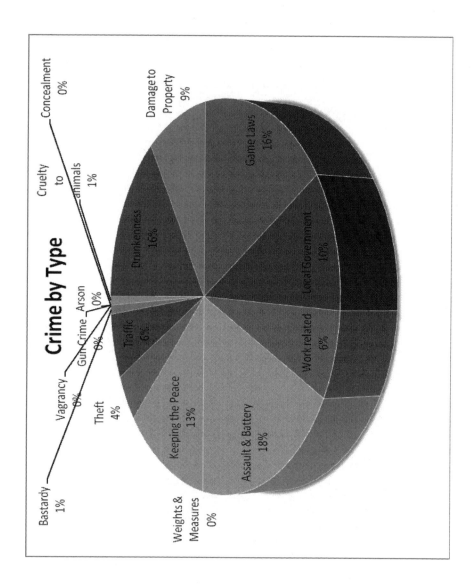

Crime by Type

- Concealment 0%
- Damage to Property 9%
- Game Laws 16%
- Cruelty to animals 1%
- Drunkenness 16%
- Local Government 10%
- Arson 0%
- Gun Crime 0%
- Work related 6%
- Traffic 6%
- Vagrancy 0%
- Theft 4%
- Keeping the Peace 13%
- Assault & Battery 18%
- Bastardy 1%
- Weights & Measures 0%

The number of cases classified by type shows that Assault cases (18%) were the most common type of offence closely followed by Drunkenness (16%)and Poaching (16%). Petty thefts were quite rare (4%).

Not all cases resulted in guilty verdicts. The actual outcomes of the year's cases are shown below.

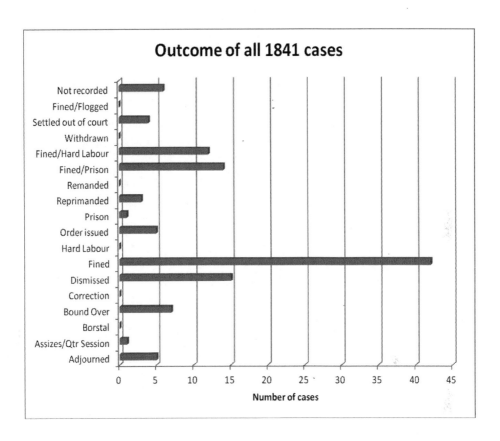

In as many as 42 cases (40%) there was a fine imposed whilst a further 26 cases were given a fine which if not paid would result in imprisonment with or without hard labour.

The fines are made up of several components:

- The value of any damage done to a victim's property

- The value of any costs to witnesses / the constable

- A punitive fine to deter a repeat offence

In some cases the records show the detailed breakdown of any fine but in many cases there is only one monetary amount plus a statement that it includes costs.

Those cases where a sentence of 'Fine or Prison' is recorded in the Court Minutes is generally not formally resolved i.e. it is quite unusual for the court record to state whether the fine was actually paid. We can only assume that, if the defendant was not subsequently subject to a warrant/order to reappear before the court, they had indeed paid the fine. There were however two cases where the defendant, when presumably failing to pay the fine, was seen to reappear before the court. The first was Benjamin Poole of Pavenham, the son of the School Master, who was prosecuted by PC Neal for Assault and he eventually served 2 months hard labour. The second was Charles Costin, an Agricultural labourer, who was prosecuted for poaching by one the Felmersham farmers named Pain (Thomas or Joseph?); he eventually served 3 months in prison.

A cross reference to the Bedford Gaol database surprisingly shows that only one of these 26 cases, that of Benjamin Poole, resulted in imprisonment.

A cross reference to police records showed that non-payment of a fine by John Johnson from Turvey resulted in him spending 6 hours in the stock at Odell . This case was from Bedford Division hence not in the Bletsoe records.

Only 1 case was escalated to the Quarter Session / Assizes but there is no record of the BUTLER case in the Quarter Session database. The case was brought by James Harris the parish constable at Harrold but there is no BUTLER living at Harrold within the census data. We must assume that he or she was passing through Harrold and that it was an unplanned theft. The Bedford Gaol database also has no record for a BUTLER prisoner in 1841.

The result of an independent search of the Gaol Database gives a different perspective on crime in North Bedfordshire.

The search on 'residence' and 'place of birth' fields using village names from within the Bletsoe Division shows that 19 of the 269 records for 1841 were from our area. The very first entry for the calendar year is for a case against John Godley for stealing a linen shirt value 2s 6d.

Gaol Record Detail For: John Godley

Record ID:	6572
Commital Year:	1841
Reference Doc:	BLARS QGV10/2
ID in Reference Doc:	741
Age:	22
Gender:	Male
Height:	5 feet 10 inches
Hair Colour:	Brown
Eye Colour:	Light hazel
Complexion:	pale
Identifying Features:	Well looking
Education:	Read and Write Imperfectly
Birth Town:	Bolnhurst
Birth County:	Bedfordshire
Residence(town/village):	Bolnhurst
Residence(county):	Bedfordshire
Offence:	Stealing A Shirt
Committed By:	W.H.Wade Gery Esquire
When Committed:	01/01/1841
Trial Session:	Epiphany 1841
Type of Gaol:	Bedford, New House of Correction
Sentence:	8 Months Hard Labour
General Remarks on Prisoner:	Indifferent

The court records do not include any details from a session on January 1st hence this case does not in appear in our analysis . The Gaol records do differ from the Quarter Session records; the latter shows a sentence of only 3 months. The QS depositions do include a description of how resident in Bolnhurst chased after the 'travelling man' and detained him after some resistance. He was held in the public house whilst the constable was summoned. He escaped through a window before being recaptured.

The second entry from our area is for a William RANDALL for a case of Assault in Colmworth. There is a corresponding court record for that date for a defendant named READWELL who was only given a fine of 15s with 9s costs. Presumably it was not paid and he was subsequently sentenced to 1 month in prison.

There are then 4 consecutive cases showing the extent of a riot at Harrold

Gaol Record Detail For: Thomas Panter

Record ID:	6681
Commital Year:	1841
Reference Doc:	BLARS QGV10/2
ID in Reference Doc:	851
Age:	36
Gender:	male
Height:	5 feet 11 inches
Hair Colour:	Brown
Eye Colour:	Hazel
Complexion:	Fresh
Identifying Features:	Very stout made large bones
Education:	Read Imperfectly
Birth Town:	Harrold
Birth County:	Bedfordshire
Residence(town/village):	Harrold
Residence(county):	Bedfordshire
Offence:	Assault
Committed By:	Rev.V.Alston and Rev.H.D.Ward
When Committed:	31/05/1841
Type of Gaol:	Bedford County Gaol
Sentence:	2 Calendar Months or pay 6 pounds 5 shillings
Discharge Date:	30/07/1841
General Remarks on Prisoner:	Orderly

Gaol Record Detail For: William Allen

Record ID:	6682
Commital Year:	1841
Reference Doc:	BLARS QGV10/2
ID in Reference Doc:	852
Age:	19
Gender:	Male
Height:	5 feet 4½ inches
Hair Colour:	Brown
Eye Colour:	Hazel
Complexion:	Fresh
Identifying Features:	Scar over left eye
Education:	Neither
Birth Town:	Harrold
Birth County:	Bedfordshire
Residence(town/village):	Harrold
Residence(county):	Bedfordshire
Offence:	Rioting
Committed By:	Rev.V.Alston and Rev.H.D.Ward
When Committed:	31/05/1841
Type of Gaol:	Bedford, New House of Correction
Sentence:	3 Months
General Remarks on Prisoner:	Orderly

Record ID:	6683
Commital Year:	1841
Reference Doc:	BLARS QGV10/2
ID in Reference Doc:	853
Age:	33
Gender:	Male
Height:	6 feet 0 inches
Hair Colour:	Brown
Eye Colour:	Hazel
Complexion:	Fresh
Identifying Features:	Very stout made
Education:	Read Imperfectly
Birth Town:	Harrold
Birth County:	Bedfordshire
Residence(town/village):	Harrold
Residence(county):	Bedfordshire
Offence:	Riot and Rescue
Committed By:	Rev.V.Alston and Rev.H.D.Wa
When Committed:	31/05/1841
Trial Session:	Midsummer 1841
Type of Gaol:	Bedford, New House of Correc
Sentence:	1 Month and fine 2 pounds

For **Sergeant Panter**

Record ID:	6684
Commital Year:	1841
Reference Doc:	BLARS QGV10/2
ID in Reference Doc:	854
Age:	22
Gender:	Male
Height:	5 feet 7 inches
Hair Colour:	Brown
Eye Colour:	Grey
Complexion:	Fresh
Identifying Features:	Mole left cheek
Education:	Neither
Birth Town:	Harrold
Birth County:	Bedfordshire
Residence(town/village):	Harrold
Residence(county):	Bedfordshire
Offence:	Riot and Rescue
Committed By:	Rev.V.Alston and Re
When Committed:	31/05/1841
Trial Session:	Midsummer 1841
Trial Verdict:	Acquitted
Type of Gaol:	Bedford County Ga

For **Thomas Matthews**

The census data shows Sergeant Panter to be a brother of Thomas and he was leading a group of men who were trying to prevent Thomas from being arrested by PC Neal with assistance from Harrold Parish Constable James Harris. The records show that Sergeant Panter was never again imprisoned in Bedford Gaol however Thomas Panter was subsequently convicted for 1 month for assault at Harrold in 1849. Thomas Matthews was acquitted of rioting and never again seen in the gaol records.

The Quarter Session records show 4 other persons (William Baulk; John Wright; John Goodman; Joseph Maunders)-were also involved in the riot, but never appeared in the gaol records, because they were also acquitted of the charge of assaulting a peace officer in the execution of his office.

On the other hand, William Allen served 3 months for rioting at Odell and was bound over for £20 to keep the peace for 6 months. This was just the first step as he was to serve two later sentences; one in 1852 for assaulting PC Charles Barker for which he served 3 weeks hard labour and again in 1856 for assaulting the police and resisting arrest when he served 2 months hard labour. The gaol record of his identifying features reads like a history of violence

Identifying Features: Cut mark on forehead, cut mark corner of right eye, cut mark on nose, blue mark right of nose, cut mark left side upper lip, lost two upper front teeth, right thumb has been broken

An assault in Harrold was also the case brought against William Drage. He was imprisoned for 2 months.

Also in July there were two cases from Wymington involving the theft of a sack and a bushel of wheat from their master Richard Longuet Orlebar. Peter Jolley, aged 54, was found guilty and sentenced to 6 months hard labour in the House of Correction whilst John Wilmer, aged 26, was acquitted. He presumably had been in Bedford gaol, awaiting his court appearance. The Quarter Session records record the former as Peter 'Jolly' which was consistent with the census.

The only case to specifically involve a Sharnbrook resident was a case against John Woods for stealing pollard for which he was sentenced to 1 year hard labour. He was a repeat offender in 1848 when he was sentenced to a further 9 moths hard labour for stealing flour from where he worked at Toft Farm.

Another case of assault was brought against John Elsom(e) from Thurleigh (born in Bolnhurst) who had attacked William Bird of Sharnbrook with a gun. He was sentenced to 1 month in Bedford County Gaol. In 1844 he was again before the Quarter Sessions and was bound on surety of £10 to keep the peace particularly towards Thomas Asplin of Thurleigh.

Late in the year William Pratt and Uriah King were prosecuted for fowl stealing. Pratt, aged 18, was acquitted but subsequently served a 6 week imprisonment for bastardy in 1845. King was also acquitted of fowl stealing but was subsequently imprisoned twice in 1844 for theft and again in 1850 for misbehaviour in the Bedford Workhouse. The misdemeanour heard in the Bedford Division court was detailed as 'whistling in the dining room when told not to' and he was sentenced to 3 weeks in prison. The final part of the story which will be seen in the next chapter was yet another acquittal for fowl stealing in Harrold in 1851.

Did the cases held in Sharnbrook Petty Session get into the local press? The local newspapers of this period were very different from today. The Bedfordshire Mercury and Huntingdon Express typically included several pages on national stories with particular emphasis on royalty, politics and major infrastructure issues. It often included lengthy reports of notorious murder cases. Other pages focussed on local issues and regularly gave full reports of the Assizes. Reports of Petty Session were less common but did include Newport Pagnell, Woburn, Ampthill, Huntingdon, Hitchin and Stony Stratford i.e. more reports from Buckinghamshire than Bedfordshire. In fact Bletsoe Sessions were not reported at all until October 2nd, which happened to be the busiest day during the year when 15 cases were heard. 8 of the cases seen in the court records were detailed in the newspaper article. There were of course inconsistencies in the defendant's names and even the crimes they were accused of. The article included a case of Drunk and Disorderly against an Archibald Howlett which did not appear in the court record.   On the other hand there were a further 7 cases in the court records which did not appear in the newspaper article.

Who had brought the case against the defendants? Using the census occupation and family relationship data it was possible to identify the nature of the prosecutor and the probable relationship to the defendant. They were classified as follows

Number of cases prosecuted by	1841
Police Constable	48
Police Sergeant	1
Police Superintendent/Inspector	2
Victim	27
Overseer of Poor	1
GameKeeper	3
Toll Keeper	1
Magistrate	2
Victim's Relative	0
Unknown	28
Informant	0
Parish Constable	2

We see that in only the second year of Rural Constabulary that Police Officers account for 51 (44%) of the cases and this figure is much higher than that for victims or victims representatives (23%). Only 2% of cases were prosecuted by the Parish Constable and the court records rarely record the Parish Constable to be even a witness for a specific case.

The overall analyses of all the above records suggest that the magistrate must have recognised two types of cases at any one session.

- Where misdemeanours are handled summarily and where a fine is the norm but often with the caveat that you will go to prison if the fine is not paid and

- Where, for more serious crimes, the defendant goes to prison to await the next Quarter Session in Bedford.

The first type of case is normally fully documented in the Court Minutes and the only failings in record keeping come when there are acquittals or adjournments. The second type of case is not always recorded in the Petty Session Minutes and there is certainly no attempt to follow through on cases and record the eventual outcome or sentence.

The performance of the County Rural Constabulary was assessed every year by Her Majesty's Inspectorate of Constabulary (HMIC) but this did not begin until after the 1856 Act which mandated all Counties to set up a formal county rural police force.

By coincidence this year also saw the creation of the Rural Constabulary in Hertfordshire. The fact that other counties close to Bedfordshire may form a full-time police force which causes criminals to migrate to Bedfordshire was highlighted during the 1839 Quarter Session discussions. In many ways the decision in Hertford was similar to Bedford and the dissenting role played in Bedford by Orlebar and St John was mirrored by The Marquis of Salisbury. He had praised the parish constable system and dwelt upon the increased costs of the proposed new force. After an amendment was rejected the vote for the new force was passed by a majority of 1.

Chapter Four: 1851

The previous decade had seen many significant political struggles across Europe. 1848 had been the year of Revolution and more than half of the nations in Europe had undergone some level of revolution. The French revolution was driven by nationalist and republican ideals among the French general public, who believed the people should rule themselves. It ended the constitutional monarchy of Louis-Philippe, and led to the creation of the French Second Republic. The revolutions were most important in France, the Netherlands, Germany, Poland, Italy, and the Austrian Empire, but did not reach Russia, Sweden, Great Britain, and most of southern Europe (Spain, Serbia, Greece, Montenegro and Portugal).

The European Potato Failure was a food crisis caused by potato blight that struck Northern Europe in the mid-1840s. The time is therefore also known as the Hungry Forties. While the crisis produced excess mortality and suffering across the affected areas, particularly affected were the Scottish Highlands and, even more harshly, Ireland. Many people starved due to lack of access to other staple food sources. The effect of the crisis on Ireland was incomparable to all other places, causing one million deaths, up to two million refugees, and spurring a century-long population decline.

On the other hand, the 1842 government report on living conditions resulted in improvements to water supply and drainage and also introduced local health officers.

Sir Robert Peel, Tory, had been the prime minister between 1841 – 1846. Peel's second term was nothing short of tumultuous. It featured economic depression, rising deficits, Chartist agitation, famine in Ireland and Anti-Corn League protests. A set of legislation was created to stabilise the economy and improve working conditions. The Factory Act regulated work hours (and banned children under eight from the workplace), the Railway Act provided for cheap, regular train services, the Bank Charter Act capped the number of notes the Bank of England could issue and the Mines Act prevented women and children from working underground. A failed harvest in 1845 provided Peel with his greatest challenge. There was an increasing clamour for repeal of the Corn Laws, which forbade the import of cheap grain from overseas. Powerful vested interests in the Tory Party opposed such a move, but in the end Peel confronted them and called for repeal. After nearly six months of debate and with the Tories split in two, the Corn Laws were finally repealed.

The only other Prime minister in this period was Lord John Russell, a younger son of the 6th Duke of Bedford. Earl Russell, a Whig, was prime minister 1846 - 1851

Confronted by the Irish Potato Famine, declining trade and rising unemployment, Russell still managed to push through trade liberalisation measures and limits on women's working hours. A dedicated reformer, he nonetheless presided over the rejection of the Third Chartist Petition. Set out 1838, it demanded universal male suffrage (votes for all adult men), secret ballots (rather than traditional open ballots), annual parliamentary elections, equal electoral districts (some had less than 500 voters, while others had many thousands), the abolition of a property qualification for members of parliament (MPs), and payment for MPs (which would allow non-independently wealthy men to sit in parliament). Already rejected once by parliament in 1839, the petition had gathered 5 million signatures by 1848. Presented to parliament a second time, it was again rejected. The Chartist movement slowly petered out, even as revolutions blazed across Europe, but many of its aims were eventually realised.

The railway expansion started in the 1830s grew so that by this time a vast, sprawling network of railways was built all around the British Isles. By 1852 there were over 7000 miles of rail track in England and Scotland, and every significant centre could now rely on rail communication. Britain's railways transformed the landscape both physically and culturally. New opportunities were produced for commerce and travel, the railways literally paving the way for industrial and economic development. Trains transported goods around the world at unprecedented rates and British technologies and engineers were responsible for railway construction across the Empire, in the Americas and in many part of Europe. The prospect of London based criminals using the railways to commit crimes in Bedfordshire and then escape back to the metropolis had been a factor in the 1839 discussions about setting up the Rural Constabulary. The actual building of the railways led to problems as the navvies had to have encampments and crime, particularly thefts and assaults, was commonplace.

The Midland Railway was formed from 3 other companies in 1844, but did not have its own route to London, and relied upon a junction at Rugby with the London and Birmingham's line to London Euston for access to the capital. By the 1850s the junction at Rugby had become severely congested so the Midland Railway constructed a direct route from Leicester to Hitchin via Sharnbrook and Bedford giving access to London via the Great Northern Railway from Hitchin.

Nationally we have seen the introduction of Police Detectives in London and the recruitment of a large number of Special Constables. The latter was a response to the concern by the people who owned property that the Chartists activity might indeed lead to revolution. 1842 also saw the opening of the new model prison at Pentonville. Several years later we saw changes in sentencing e.g. the beginning of solitary confinement and the gradual end of transportation.

Locally, William Byers Graham was still the Superintendent at Bletsoe Division in 1851 and the first Sergeant had been appointed to the Division in 1850. There were now three levels of Police Constable and the pay structure reflected this. By 1851 Graham was also appointed High Constable for the Hundreds thus further absorbing responsibility for the role of Parish Constables.

All of the local concerns about the increasing costs of the new constabulary had been suppressed.

The second of the national censuses was held on the 30th March 1851 and Sharnbrook's registrar was again John Williamson and the enumerator was Thomas Peck. The census return on 190 schedules showed 888 residents, an increase of 5% from the 1841 survey. The gender distribution was 437 males and 451 females; 287 (32%) were under the age of 14. This total represented the high point for Sharnbrook's population in the 19thC.

Sharnbrook was still only the third most populated village in North Beds. The highest population was still in Harrold which had continued to grow. However some 42% of the villages were experiencing a decrease in population since 1841.

A Post Office Receiving House had been created in Sharnbrook in 1843 and the cart deliver mail from Bedford for collection at Sharnbrook. There was no delivery of post to individual houses at this time.

The 1851 total population across all the villages covered by the Bletsoe Division was 14,611.

The Sharnbrook tradesmen now included one Baker, two Blacksmiths, two bootmakers, three butchers, one miller, two tailors, a grocer, a saddler, two drapers, a plumber, two stonemasons, a watchmaker, a wheelwright and a surgeon. There were also two publicans, a beer retailer, a builder, a hairdresser, a glass and china dealer and a vicar, a Baptist minister and three school masters/mistresses.

In addition the census showed 143 agricultural labourers, 40 skilled agricultural occupations and 84 in domestic service.

During the entirety of 1851 the Petty Sessions were held by one or more of only 7 magistrates

Lord St John	Wade- Geary	Orlebar	Higgins
Rev CC Beatty-Pownall	HW Beauford	Rev V Alston	

According to the Petty Session Minutes the most cases were heard by Wade-Geary (110) closely followed by Beatty-Pownall (99). Alston was present for the fewest number of cases (only 1, which was recorded as an extraordinary session).

The cases were distributed across the year

Jan - Mar	Apr- Jun	Jul- Sep	Oct - Dec	Total
38	37	57	22	154

The highest number of case in any one session was again 15.

The Minutes were still written in a non-structured format and the information was not always complete or consistent. The standard of data recording had slightly improved since all cases did record the nature of the crime and some now recorded where the crime had been committed.

Had the level and type of crime changed?

The number of cases in 1851 classified by type

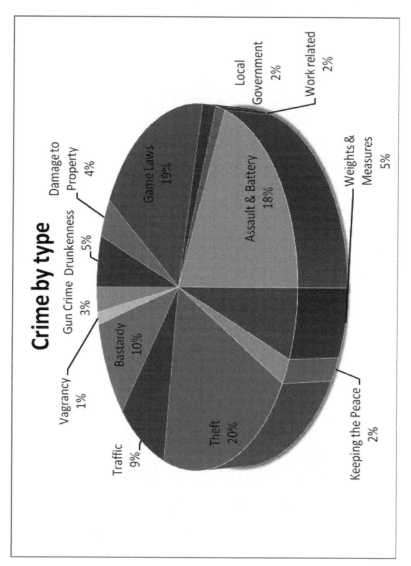

Crime by type

Local Government 2%
Work related 2%
Weights & Measures 5%
Assault & Battery 18%
Game Laws 19%
Damage to Property 4%
Drunkenness 5%
Gun Crime 3%
Vagrancy 1%
Bastardy 10%
Traffic 9%
Theft 20%
Keeping the Peace 2%

Assault cases remained at 18% but are no longer the most common type of offence ; that position is now taken by Theft at 20% closely followed by

Game Law offences also at 19%. This reflects a six-fold increase in thefts since 1841.

Not all cases resulted in guilty verdicts. The actual outcomes of the year's cases are shown

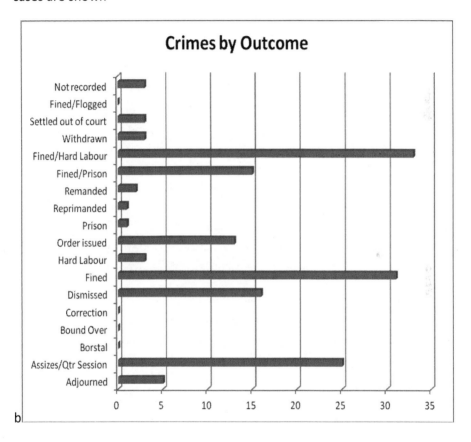

Imposition of a fine was again customary with as many as 31 cases (20%) where there was a fine imposed whilst a further 48 cases were given a fine which if not paid would result in imprisonment with or without hard labour.

The details of the fines continue to show a breakdown into similar components:

- The value of any damage done to a victim's property or the plaintiff's costs

- The value of any costs to witnesses / the constable

- A punitive fine to deter a repeat offence

The cases where a sentence of 'Fine or Prison' is recorded in the Court Minutes are generally not formally resolved i.e. it was still quite unusual for the court record to state whether the fine was actually paid.

In the 25 cases that were escalated to the Quarter Session/ Assizes we can see that only 8 of these cases appeared in the subsequent Quarter Session listings. They included Moses Wooding who had been prosecuted by the Overseer of the Poor in Wymington and had been found guilty of Vagrancy and Neglect of his family but who was pardoned of the vagrancy offence at the Quarter Session.

At the Quarter Session Tom Fairey had pleaded guilty to stealing a drainage tool and spade at Dean and was sentenced to 3 weeks in prison. Charles Page was later sentenced to a similar offence at Keysoe and was given a 2 months prison sentence. The gaol database recorded this as 2 months hard labour.

Late in the year three offenders, Levi Allen, Eli Allen and George Prentice, were all accused of stealing 5 gallons of ale from the Colworth estate. They were all found guilty and sentenced to 3 months in prison. Levi and Eli were both carpenters living in Sharnbrook. Levi , still only aged 25, was the father of 4 children.

The longest sentence seen in the QS record is for Ann Guess who was accused of stealing a pair of gold studs, a comb, a pairs of scissors and other articles from Sarah Chettle at Shelton. She was found guilty and sentenced to 4 months in prison. The Gaol database shows it as 4 months hard labour.

For this year we start to see a greater proportion of the cases reflected in the Gaol database.

At the beginning of the year we see Thomas and Jacob Asplin, from Thurleigh, accused of Night Poaching at Sharnbrook. This was Jacob's first court appearance for Game Law offences whilst Thomas had been a repeat offender since 1843. Jacob was given a 1 month hard labour sentence but Thomas received 10 months with hard labour. Jacob was already in domestic service by the 1841 census so it is not clear if they are related.

In total, 42 of the 154 cases in the court records were in the Gaol Database. These do include people who were held in gaol awaiting trial and subsequently acquitted as well as offenders who were found guilty and sentenced to long periods in the prison. The former include Uriah King who was acquitted of fowl stealing in both 1841 and 1851.

One of the few examples of whipping was seen in January with the conviction of the juvenile, John Munton Roe. John was found guilty of stealing 1.5d from the Revd Mudge in Pertenhall and was sentenced to 1 week hard labour plus a whipping. There is no record of him re-offending.

Gaol Record Detail For: John Roe

Record ID:	9835
Commital Year:	1851
Reference Doc:	BLARS QGV10/3
ID in Reference Doc:	962
Age:	12
Gender:	Male
Height:	4 feet 7 inches
Hair Colour:	Brown
Eye Colour:	Grey
Complexion:	Fresh
Visage:	Round
Identifying Features:	Teeth very irregular in front of mouth
Occupation:	Labourer
Education:	Neither
Marital Status:	Single
Birth Town:	Wilsthorp
Residence(town/village):	Pertenhall
Residence(county):	Bedfordshire
Offence:	On 5th Jan.1851 at Pertenhall being of the age of 12 years stealing one and a half pence the monies goods and chattels of the Rev.Wiliam Mudge
Committed By:	Lord St.John and Rev.C.C.B.Pownall
When Committed:	21/01/1851
Trial Type:	Summarily Convicted
Type of Gaol:	Bedford County Gaol
Sentence:	1 Week Hard Labour Gaol and once privately whipped
Discharge Date:	27/01/1851

Another example of a single time offender is Owen Mackness from Wymington who was convicted of trespassing in the day time on land of Alfred Manning in search of Game. He was sentenced to 3 weeks hard labour.

In April a pair of tramps appeared at the same session accused of burglary. Samuel York, born in Hargrave, was also accused of stealing a gold ring, value £10. He had a previous conviction of assaulting a Parish Constable back in 1838. He was now convicted to 10 years transportation. During the same court proceedings Samuel was committed for trial at the Quarter Session for stealing a horse from William Rose. Samuel York was with 234 other convicts on the ship 'Dudbrook' when it sailed from Plymouth to the Swan River Colony, Western Australia in November 1852. Strangely, the convict record, register no. 1550, shows Samuel's offence to be arson. This mistake is because the two previous registration numbers are for two other offenders from Bedford, John Emmerton and Thomas Gower, who both received 10 years for arson.(1)

An identical sentence was passed for William Morris who was accused of breaking and entering the house of Thomas Medlow at Little Staughton and stealing 2 Shawls and other things. After being found guilty and removed to Millbank, William Morris sailed on the same ship as Samuel York and they landed in Western Australia after 77 days at sea in February 1853. The 600 ton ship had been captained by John Innes. There were no female convicts on board. The convict record correctly shows his offence to be burglary. The records from the ship's surgeon , Charles Keveru, shows William to be aged 34, labourer, single, 5'9", black hair, blue eyes and lists his distinguishing marks as 'Scar on right eye; forefinger left hand injured'.

Less than 10,000 offenders were transported to Western Australia between 1850 and 1868. This is small compared with even the circa 67,000 sent to Van Diemen's Land earlier in the century. 5% of all transportations to Australia were for offenders convicted of burglary. Theft was the most common offence equating to 17% of all transportations. There had been 16 sailings of transport ships during 1852; this compared with 31 sailings at its peak in

1829. The year where there were the greatest number of transportations was 1834 when nearly 5000 people were transported. 84% of all transportees were male. The average conviction was 9 years but of the estimated 160,000 convicts some 28,000 received life sentences.

Returning to the Gaol database we see that in May we have a conviction of James Day for assault on the Police Superintendent William Byers Graham. Day, an agricultural labourer born in Sharnbrook, had a previous conviction for assault in 1842 when he served a 2 month sentence. He was now sentenced to only 14 days probably because Graham had given evidence explaining the circumstances of the event suggesting some degree of possibility that it was partly accidental because Day had been drunk. James Day did go on to serve two short sentences in the debtor's cells at Bedford County Gaol later in the 1850s.

Also in May we see John Pettit, who lived in Poddington, convicted of breaking and stealing pales forming part of a fence owned by Richard Orlebar. He was summarily convicted and failing to pay the fine he served 3 weeks hard labour.

In July, we have John Lucas, a shoemaker born in St Neots, appearing for two offences ; one was an assault on Joseph Carter at Yelden; the second for unlawfully using a gun to kill game. He was sentenced to 3 months hard labour. Four years later he is again convicted of a Game Law offence and he was summarily convicted to 2 months hard labour. John Auburn was also convicted of the 1851 offence of using a gun to kill game and was given the same sentence. There is no record of him re-offending.

In October we have another assault on the police. Samuel Bailey, aged 18, was accused of assaulting PC Samuel Harper at Poddington and, failing to pay the fine, served 2 months hard labour at the New House of Correction. Three years later he is convicted for stealing a pigeon from Richard Orlebar at Podington and is convicted to 3 weeks hard labour.

Gaol Record Detail For: Samuel Bailey

Record ID:	11640
Commital Year:	1854
Reference Doc:	BLARS QGV10/3
ID in Reference Doc:	2767
Age:	20
Gender:	Male
Height:	5 feet 8¼ inches
Hair Colour:	Brown
Eye Colour:	Hazel
Complexion:	Ruddy
Visage:	Oval
Identifying Features:	Burn scar on left hand
Occupation:	Labourer
Education:	None
Marital Status:	Single
Birth Town:	Podington
Birth County:	Bedfordshire
Residence(town/village):	Podington
Residence(county):	Bedfordshire
Offence:	On the 5th of December 1853 at Podington stealing a pigeon of the value of 4 pence the property of R.L.Orlebar Esquire
Committed By:	W.H.Wade Gery Esquire and John Gibbard Esquire
When Committed:	31/01/1854
Trial Type:	Summarily Convicted
Type of Gaol:	Bedford, New House of Correction
Sentence:	21 Days Hard Labour or pay 1 pound 11 shillings and 10 pence
No. of Previous Convictions:	2
Previous Conviction Details:	This prison
Discharge Date:	24/02/1854

This was the second time he had been prosecuted for stealing from the Orlebar estate; in 1850 he had served 3 weeks hard labour for stealing walnuts.

The assault on PC Harper coincided with the conviction of Bolt Partridge for an assault on PC Samuel Haynes. Partridge also from Poddington was also sentenced to 3 weeks hard labour. Nobody with the forename Bolt appears in the Bedfordshire 1851 census.

The court records show 8 convictions for Game Law offences in December and they were quite widespread i.e. Odell, Podington and Felmersham.

James York, Robert Horne and Thomas Cox all received sentences of 6 weeks hard labour.

For reasons that are not clear, the case against William Parris, hawker, was recorded in the Extraordinary Session record. He again was accused of Game Law offences, in Chellington, and was sentenced to 2 months hard labour. Also in these records was a conviction of Eli Jackson, born in Carlton, for vagrancy and deserting his family.

First Name	Last Name	Age	Committal Year	Residence/town/village	Birth Town	Offence	Sentence
Detail Eli	Jackson	31	1849	Carlton	Carlton	Stealing Wheat	3 Calendar Months Hard Labour
Detail Eli	Jackson	31	1849			Stealing Wheat	3 Calendar Months Hard Labour
Detail Eli	Jackson	31	1850			Stealing Apples	1 Calendar Month Hard Labour
Detail Eli	Jackson	31	1850	Carlton	Carlton	Stealing a quantity of apples of the value of 2 shillings and sixpence the property of George Allen of Harrold growing in an orchard belonging to said George Allen situated at Carlton	1 Calendar Month Hard Labour
Detail Eli	Jackson	33	1851	Bedford	Carlton	On 30th April 1851 at Carlton running away and leaving his wife and family chargeable to the said Parish of Carlton	2 Calendar Months Hard Labour
Detail Eli	Jackson	33	1851			ROgue and Vagabond [Leaving his family]	2 Calendar Months Hard Labour
Detail Eli	Jackson	36	1854			Stealing 4 Cauliflowers	8 weeks or pay £5.17s.0d
Detail Eli	Jackson	36	1854	Northampton Gaol	Carlton	On the 21st of May 1853 at Carlton stealing a quantity of cauliflowers of the value of sixpence the property of Joseph Francis	8 Weeks Hard Labour or pay 5 pounds 17 shillings
Detail Eli	Jackson	44	1862			Stealing Wood	7 Days Hard Labour

This was one of series of convictions which included 4 separate instances of theft.

Did the cases held in Sharnbrook Petty Session get into the local press? The local newspapers of this period had still not got into the routine of reporting cases from Bletsoe Division. Only 3 cases were included in reports and only one in detail. The case of arson against Thomas Burgess included details of events from several witnesses including Joseph Pack, a gamekeeper from Colworth. The case was escalated to the Assizes but did not proceed because the Grand Jury decided on No Bill hence the case was dropped.

Who had brought the case against the defendants? Using the 1851 census occupation and family relationship data it was possible to identify the nature of the prosecutor and the probable relationship to the defendant.

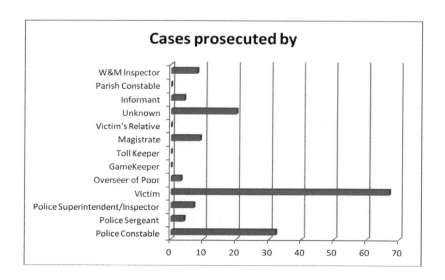

Cases prosecuted by

The proportion of cases prosecuted by the Victim has risen to 44% compared to a decrease in Police prosecutions which fell to 28% of cases (although there is an increase in cases brought specifically by the Police Superintendent). There is also an increase in case where the Magistrate is named as the plaintiff. We also start to see cases where the civil authorities are named e.g. the Weights and Measures Inspector. Since that role is now taken on by the Police Superintendent it may explain why the police prosecutions are down. There are no prosecutions by a Parish Constable. We still have not yet reached the stage where HMIC starts to conduct annual inspections of the Rural Police Force.

This particular year has the greatest number of cases escalated to the Quarter Sessions i.e. 25 of the total of 154 cases. We have seen that only 8 of these are shown in the QS record which is divergent from the Gaol database records where 42 prisoners are recorded. Of these 21 are serving Prison with hard labour hence are not just in prison awaiting trial. This number is much greater than the outcomes recorded in the Petty Session records.

References:

(1) convict records http://members.iinet.net.au/~perthdps/convicts//con-wa7.html

Chapter Five: 1861

Britain has been at war. Britain and France declare war on Russia in March 1854 and the Crimean War begins. It is concluded by the Treaty of Paris in 1856. In 1857 the power of the East India Company is challenged by the Indian Mutiny and India comes under direct British Government control.

A cholera epidemic led to demands for a clean water supply and proper sewage systems in the big cities. Cholera had been one of the major causes of death in the Crimea.

Charles Darwin's work 'On the Origin of Species' is published. Charles Dickens novels are published throughout the decade and his stories serve to highlight poor living standards in the country.

The politics in this period is extremely volatile. Lord John Russell's Whig administration collapses, in1851 and **Lord Derby** follows him as a Conservative prime minister at the head of a short-lived coalition government.

Within the same year **Lord Aberdeen**, leader of the 'Peelite' minority of the Conservative party, forms a new coalition government with the Liberals.

Lord Palmerston then heads another coalition government in Britain after Lord Aberdeen loses a vote of confidence on his conduct of the Crimean War.

In 1858 Palmerston's government collapses and Lord Derby heads another Conservative minority administration. Finally, in 1859, Liberal leader Lord Palmerston returns to office as the British prime minister after the collapse of Derby's coalition government.

Henry Bessemer invented the blast furnace hence finding a way to convert pig iron into steel, which was both stronger and lighter than iron. This made it possible to build huge structures such as bridges and ships.
Brunel's 'Great Eastern', the largest ship yet built, was launched in 1858.

Nationally we have seen the establishment of Rural Policing across all Counties. The 1856 County and Borough Police Act mandated that all counties have a formal full-time rural police force. Bedfordshire were already ahead of the game and had been one of the counties to take the opportunity offered in 1839. This still did not mean that existing Borough forces had to merge with the new County forces. This was not to happen for nearly another 100 years. The Act did however set up a mechanism for setting and controlling standards across the different police forces. The Act created an independent audit process called 'Her Majesties Inspectorate of Constabulary' (HMIC). They were actioned to conduct annual inspections of each force and to report their findings and recommendations. In 1860 the Metropolitan Police force took over the policing of all major docks across the country.

Transportation to Tasmania (1)Penal Servitude Acts, 1853 & 1857) had come to an end and Reformatory Schools had been introduced in 1854.

In Bedfordshire the Chief Constable had ordered a survey of lock-up facilities and the absence of a Police Station and Court in the Bletsoe Division was noted. In 1859 the HMIC annual report was critical of this shortage and plans were drawn up to built a new Police Station at Bletsoe. At the time the number of cases was small and the magistrates' concerns over costs meant that the plan was dropped.

Locally, William Byers Graham was still the Superintendent at Bletsoe Division in 1861 and the second Sergeant had been appointed to the Division at Riseley in 1860. The superintendent's interest in poetry culminated in his publishing a book of his own poems called 'Country Musings' with financial help provided by Lord St John.

The third of the national censuses was held on the 7th April 1861 and Sharnbrook's registrar was George Whitney and the enumerator was John Doughty. The census return on 204 schedules showed 870 residents, a decrease of 2% from the 1851 survey. The gender distribution was 431 males and 439 females; 272 (31%) were under the age of 14. Sharnbrook was still only the third most populated village in North Beds. The highest population was still in Harrold which had continued to grow. However some 62% of the villages were experiencing a decrease in population since 1851.

The 1861 total population across all the villages covered by the Bletsoe Division was slightly increased at 14,654.

The Sharnbrook tradesmen now included one postmaster, two Bakers, two Blacksmiths, two boot makers, one butchers, a grocer, a saddler, two drapers, one cattle dealer, one carpenter, two plumbers, one stonemason, five farmers, two corn merchants, a wheelwright and a surgeon. There were also two publicans, a builder, a vicar, a Baptist minister and a school master.

In addition the census showed 131 agricultural labourers, 38 skilled agricultural occupations and 105 in domestic service.

During the first three quarters of 1861 the Petty Sessions were held by one or more of 8 magistrates.

Lord St John	Wade- Geary	Orlebar	Alston
Beatty-Pownall	Starry (often spelt Starey)	J Tucker	J Gibbard

According to the Petty Session Minutes the most cases were heard by Gibbard (86) closely followed by Wade –Geary (68) and Orlebar (67). Alston was again present for the fewest number of cases. (See later comment on Police Register which explains why data is incomplete in this year).

The cases were distributed across the year

Jan - Mar	Apr- Jun	Jul- Sep	Oct - Dec	Total
48	44	39	13	144

The highest number of case in any one session was 14.

The Minutes were still written in a non-structured format and the information was not always complete or consistent. The standard of data recording had slightly improved since all cases did record the nature of the crime and some now recorded where the crime had been committed.

The end of this particular book is reached in August 1861. The first record in the new book is January 1862 hence there is some missing court data.

To overcome this we have used the Police records available under within the Police Register (2). Here, details on the magistrates serving at each session are not recorded but the details of in which village the crime occurred is certainly better recorded.

The number of cases in 1861 classified by type

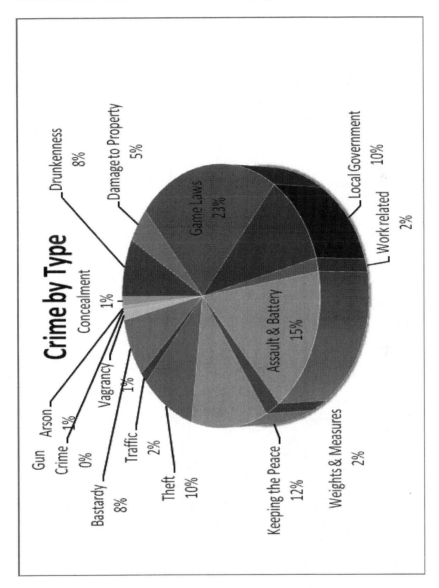

Crime by Type

Drunkenness 8%
Damage to Property 5%
Game Laws 23%
Local Government 10%
Work related 2%
Concealment 1%
Vagrancy 1%
Gun Crime 0%
Arson 1%
Traffic 2%
Bastardy 8%
Theft 10%
Keeping the Peace 12%
Assault & Battery 15%
Weights & Measures 2%

Assault cases account for 15% but they are no longer the most common type of offence ; that position is now taken by Game Law offences at 23%. This shows yet another increase in Poaching since 1851. We do see a dramatic increase in cases categorised as Local Government; these include non-payment of tolls, failing to repair roads, breaking licensing laws etc.

Not all cases resulted in guilty verdicts. The actual outcomes of the year's cases are shown :

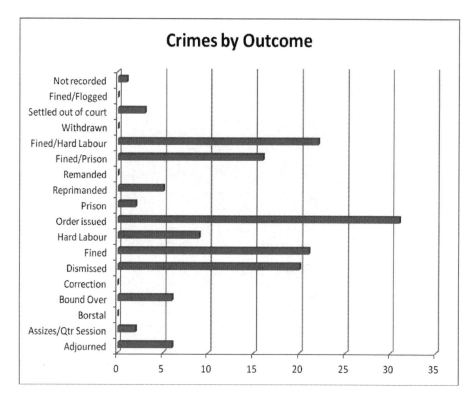

Imposition of a fine was again prevalent with as many as 21 cases (15%) where was a fine imposed whilst a further 38 cases were given a fine which if not paid would result in imprisonment with or without hard labour.

The details of the fines continue to show a breakdown into the same three components:

- The value of any damage done to a victim's property/ the plaintiff's costs

- The value of any costs to witnesses / the constable

- A punitive fine to deter a repeat offence

The cases where a sentence of 'Fine or Prison' is recorded in the Court Minutes are generally still not formally resolved although the police records do sometimes indicate the fined was paid.

The number of cases that were escalated to the Quarter Session/ Assizes is dramatically less than in 1851. There were in fact only two cases where the Court record shows the case was sent to Quarter Session / Assizes. The first case in January involved the concealment of a birth by Ann Pickering, aged 17, from Swineshead. She was bailed at a cost of £40 to appear at the higher court. The Gaol database shows that she appeared before Lord St John and R Hawley at the Assizes in March and was acquitted.

The second case was brought by S Day, a Parish Officer, against the Surveyor of Highways (unnamed) for non-repair of the road at Bolnhurst. The case is not seen in the Quarter Session records or in the Gaol database. Several months earlier in July we had seen a case relating to the repair of the road in Bolnhurst. This time the defendants were James Sharman and William Green. Court Orders were created instructing them to take action.

The Gaol database is again a very useful source because it shows entries relating to 14 of the 144 cases.

At the beginning of the year we see James Wildman, aged 48, accused of stealing two roots of mangold wurzel , value 7d. He was summarily convicted to 2 months hard labour. He was in gaol during the census and the transcript of that record shows he was born in New York, USA but the original page shows he is a tailor who was born in more modest Bletsoe!

In March we see two people accused of stealing a sheet from Susannah Brown. Charles Henry Seymour, aged 35, was convicted to 2 months hard labour whilst Matilda Davis, aged 23, received 1 month hard labour.

Gaol Record Detail For: Edward Peacock

Record ID:	38244
Commital Year:	1861
Reference Doc:	BLARS QGV15/2
ID in Reference Doc:	38
Age:	42
Gender:	Male
Height:	5 feet 10 inches
Hair Colour:	Grey
Eye Colour:	Grey
Complexion:	Fair
Identifying Features:	Proportionate
Occupation:	Miller
Education:	Read and Write
Marital Status:	Married
Amount of Debt:	£10.8.3
Birth Town:	Kimbolton
Birth County:	Huntingdonshire
Residence(town/village):	Keysoe Mill
Residence(county):	Bedfordshire
Committed By:	Bedford County Court
When Committed:	14/03/1861
Type of Gaol:	Debtors cells, Bedford County Gaol
Sentence:	20 days
How Disposed:	Clerk's Order
Discharge Date:	09/09/1861
General Remarks on Prisoner:	J. Dickens[Whitmore, farmer

Also in March we see two court appearances for Edward Peacock who is accused of failing to pay his rates. He is found guilty and sentenced to 20 days in a debtor's cell.

Yet again in March we see Les Brown pleading not guilty to a breach of the peace brought by PC Cook. The defendant and his co-defendant, Joseph Solesbury, were both bound over, the former for 6 months for £10 plus 17s costs and the latter for 3 months plus 11s expenses. Brown had boasted that he was the 'best science man in Bletsoe'.

Later we see Samuel Pettit convicted for 3 weeks for an assault on a Police Constable. He had one previous conviction for wounding a horse back in 1847 when he served 6 weeks hard labour.

In August William Line, aged 69, was convicted of stealing 11 hens eggs, value 7d. He was sentenced to 7 days hard labour. He had one previous conviction for stealing onions some 16 years earlier.

In one session at the end of August there were 7 men accused of Game Law offences by two land owners. Three of the accused received fines or 2 months hard labour, another three received the same fine or 6 weeks hard labour and one, William Barwick, had a lesser fine or 3 weeks hard labour. The Gaol database does show that Barwick, aged 22, was later convicted of a similar crime in 1862 and had to then serve 3 months hard labour.

In September John Higgins, aged 39, was convicted of stealing two brass candlesticks in Harrold. He was sentenced to 7 days hard labour. He had previously had one conviction which he served in Northampton Borough gaol.

The Gaol database shows the conviction of a juvenile offender in September; Richard Burgess, aged 14, was found guilty of stealing 5 hens eggs, value 3d. His sentence was 7 days hard labour. His wife Ann was accused of receiving the stolen eggs but that case was dismissed. The same 7 day sentence was given to John Bull who was summarily convicted of Neglect of his family.

At the end of the year we see the first of the Game Law offences committed by Michael French at Poddington. Over the following 8 years he was committed on another 3 occasions and the sentence was increasingly severe.

Total records found 4 : Page 1 of 1

	First Name	Last Name	Age	Commital Year	Residence(town/village)	Birth Town	Offence	Sentence	Document Ref
Detail	Michael	French	21	1861			Game Laws	3 Calendar Months Hard Labour	BLARS QGV12/1
Detail	Michael	French	24	1864			Game Laws	2 Calendar Months Hard Labour or pay £2.14.0	BLARS QGV12/1
Detail	Michael	French	25	1864			Game Laws	2 Calendar Months Hard Labour or pay £3.6.0	BLARS QGV12/1
Detail	Michael	French	28	1869			Stealing Fowls	6 Calendar Months Hard Labour	BLARS QGV12/2

Did the cases held in Bletsoe Petty Session get into the local press? The answer is definitely YES. It is this decade which is the watershed and cases from 19 of the 24 sessions were reported. The total number of cases reported was 88 (61%). Many of the reports just summarised the case by describing the defendant, the nature of the offence and the outcome. However in a few cases the report included a very full description of the crime scene, the witness statements and the social background of the defendant and their family.

The sad case of Elizabeth Ann Pickering is a prime example. It describes how she is accused of concealing the birth of a female child. The child was actually discovered in a ditch at Swineshead by the 17 year old girl's father, William, who had not known she was expecting a child. She had been working as a domestic servant and lived away from the family home. The doctor's report had confirmed there were no marks of violence on the child's body. He was not able to swear the baby had been born alive. After an adjournment the report describes witness reports and the defendants evidence which described how she was not able to take the child's body back to her family home through fear of 'upsetting her mother's mind'. Elizabeth was committed for trial. A subsequent newspaper report confirms that she pleaded not guilty. The indictment was dismissed on a point of law because there was no evidence of any attempt to actually conceal, i.e. secretly bury, the child's body. The judge ordered the jury to find the prisoner Not Guilty. She was accordingly discharged.

The report of the cases against George Brown of Bletsoe and Joseph Solesbury of Milton Ernest showed how Brown's boast of being the 'best scienced man in Bletsoe' had led to the fight between the two men. Brown had claimed that Solesbury had assaulted him first and had torn 3 buttons off his waistcoat. It noted that since Brown had previously appeared in court he received a more severe fine and was bound over for a longer period.

A more serious and organised fight between two men at Colmworth was also described in detail. The affray resulted in 4 separate cases. John Howkins, farmer in Colmworth, and Thomas Miles, a labourer from Little Staughton, were charged with fighting. The police also charged their two seconds, Samuel Fensom and Thomas Briers. The quarrel originated at the Wheat Sheaf Inn where they had been drinking. Howkins, Miles and Briers were bound over in £10 to keep the peace for 6 months; Fensom, who had taken a less active part, was let off with costs of 2s. Lord St John gave them all a caution and advised Howkins not to frequent the public house.

Who had brought the case against the defendants? Using the 1861 census occupation and family relationship data it was possible to identify the nature of the prosecutor and the probable relationship to the defendant.

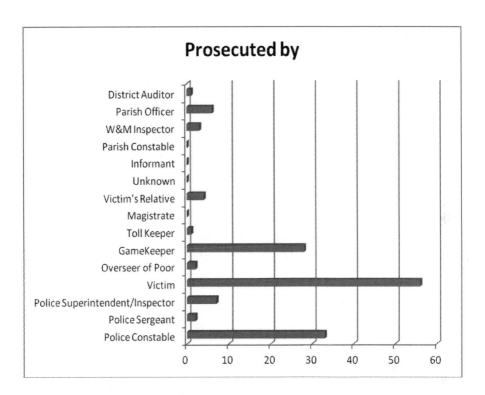

Prosecuted by

The number of cases prosecuted by the Victim has fallen to 56 (39%) whilst the proportion of case brought by a police officer remains constant at 29%. Reflecting the fact that Game Law crimes are now the most prevalent we start to see prosecutions by a Gamekeeper. The gamekeeper is now named as the plaintiff, rather than the landowner, in 28 cases (20% of total cases).

There are still no prosecutions by a Parish Constable.

We have now reached the stage where HMIC starts to conduct annual inspections of the Rural Police Force. The report for 1861 showed the strength of the force as 75 i.e. 1 chief constable, 1 deputy chief constable, 6 superintendents, 8 serjeants, 31 first class, 22 second class and 6 third class constables. The report showed a continuing commitment against public houses and beer houses reflecting the recognition that drunkenness was a key factor in many crimes. The report indicated that 685 thieves and 485 suspected persons lived in the county, being a proportion of 19 to every 1 police constable. It specifically mentions the Bletsoe Magistrates' view that a new police station is not required but states that they still think a small second class station would add to the efficiency of the Division as, over the year, 11 prisoners were kept in constable's residences, 5 at public houses and 3 were remanded to Bedford. Overall the force was described as efficient.

This particular year has the fewest number of cases in the court records escalated to the Quarter Sessions i.e. 2 of the total of 144 cases. We have seen that none of these are shown in the QS record but they are shown in both the Gaol database and the newspaper reports. A search in the BLARS catalogue using the reference 'QSR1861' shows nearly 400 hits and the Gaol database shows 523 prisoners during the year but the location data is so sparse that only 3 records relate to defendants living in the villages of Bletsoe Division.

References:

(1) Penal Servitude Acts, 1853 & 1857

(2) Police Register BLARS QER/12

.

Chapter Six: 1871

At the end of 1861 Prince Albert died, aged 42, and Queen Victoria is widowed. She withdrew from royal duties for 10 years.

The civil war in America lasts for 4 years.

In 1863 Treasury agrees to fund Ordnance Survey national mapping project. The first city underground railway project is opened in London.

The Second Reform Act virtually doubles the electorate in the UK to 2 million.

Discontent in Ireland leads to the Fenian rising.

Palmerston , Russell and Lord Derby all did further stints as prime minister.

Benjamin Disraeli was a conservative PM for a few months in 1868 but immediately lost an election to the Liberals. He had observed that 'he had reached the top of the greasy pole'.

William Gladstone started his first term as prime minister in 1868

Nationally, the Prisons Act 1865 (1) aimed to enforce a strict, uniform regime of punishment in all 193 local prisons

depriving county justices and municipal corporations of their independent authority over local gaols. The intention was not to try to reform prisoners through work or religion but to impose strict standards of discipline through 'hard labour, hard fare and a hard board'. This required the use of a treadmill or crank.

Transportation finally ended with the last convict ship ' Hougoumont' arrived in Western Australia on 9th January 1868. There were 281 passengers of

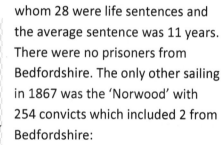

whom 28 were life sentences and the average sentence was 11 years. There were no prisoners from Bedfordshire. The only other sailing in 1867 was the 'Norwood' with 254 convicts which included 2 from Bedfordshire:

- Walter Pratt sentenced to 12 years at Bedford Assizes in 1864

- George Wade who was sentenced to 10 years at Bedford Assizes in 1865

1868 had also seen the last public execution in England i.e. the last fully public hanging was to be that of Michael Barrett at Newgate. Twenty seven year old Barrett originated in Co. Fermanagh, Ireland, and was a member of the Fenians . He was convicted of causing an explosion at the Clerkenwell House of Detention in London on the 13th of December 1867, in an attempt to free Richard O'Sullivan Burke, a Fenian Brotherhood member. The bomb blew a huge hole in the prison wall, destroying and damaging several houses opposite the prison in Corporation Lane. The blast killed seven innocent people and injured many more.

In Bedfordshire the Chief Constable had ordered a clamp down on vagrancy. The number of cases throughout the early part of the decade was about 30 per year but in 1869 there was a peak of 152 prisoners in the gaol database. This was the last project before Captain Edward Boultbee, Chief Constable, retired in 1871.

Locally, William Byers Graham, the Superintendent at Bletsoe Division was transferred to be both Superintendent of the Bedford Division and Deputy Chief Constable. He had served as Superintendent at Bletsoe for 20 years, the longest of all the senior officers in the Division. In 1871 he was invited to stay on and help with the arrival of the second Chief Constable rather than retire.

Thomas Simmonds then William Snell were short term appointments as Superintendent at Sharnbrook. In 1864 that position was given to James Carruthers who was to become the second longest serving senior officer in the Division.

One of his first cases was the conviction of harness maker **John Neale**, aged 50, for arson at Little Staughton. He had set fire to a stack of corn owned by Thomas Brightman. He was sentenced to 6 years penal servitude and was removed to Leicester County Gaol. He did not have any previous convictions.

The decision to build a police station and court house was finally made and the location would be Sharnbrook rather than Bletsoe. The building was started in 1871.

The fourth of the national censuses was held on the 2nd April 1871 and Sharnbrook's registrar was again George Whitney and the enumerator was John Thomas Dickinson. The census return on 196 schedules showed 840 residents, a decrease of 3% from the 1861 survey. The gender distribution was 409 males and 431 females; 298 (35%) were under the age of 14. Sharnbrook was now only the fourth most populated village in North Beds having fallen behind Keysoe. Keysoe's population had increased slightly in both 1861 and 1871. The highest population was still in Harrold but like Sharnbrook its population was beginning to fall. In fact some 77% of the villages were experiencing a decrease in population since 1861.

The 1871 total population across all the villages covered by the Bletsoe Division was slightly decreased at 14,346.

Using the nearest trade directory the Sharnbrook tradesmen now included one postmaster, two bakers, two Blacksmiths, two boot makers, two butchers, a saddler, two drapers, two tailors, one cattle dealer, a carpenter, two plumbers, two millers, a carrier, two builders, two stonemasons, six farmers, a watchmaker, two corn merchants, three coal merchants, a wheelwright and a surgeon. There were also two publicans and a beer retailer, a builder, a vicar, a Baptist minister and two school teachers.

In addition the census showed 141 agricultural labourers, 54 skilled agricultural occupations and 104 in domestic service.

During the entirety of 1871 the Petty Sessions were held by one or more of 7 magistrates

Lord St John	Chapman	Orlebar	SG Gillies Payne
Beatty-Pownall	Starry (often spelt Starey)	J Tucker	

According to the Petty Session Minutes the most cases were heard by St John (84) with Beatty Pownall next on 49 cases. The fewest number of cases was heard by Chapman .

The cases were distributed across the year

Jan - Mar	Apr- Jun	Jul- Sep	Oct - Dec	Total
20	56	28	19	123

The highest number of cases in any one session was 25, considerably higher than any of the previous study years.

The Minutes were now written in quite a structured format however the records are not complete and many cases were only identified by Reference to the local newspaper reports. It is therefore impossible to know the exact number of cases heard at the court.

The number of cases in 1871 classified by type

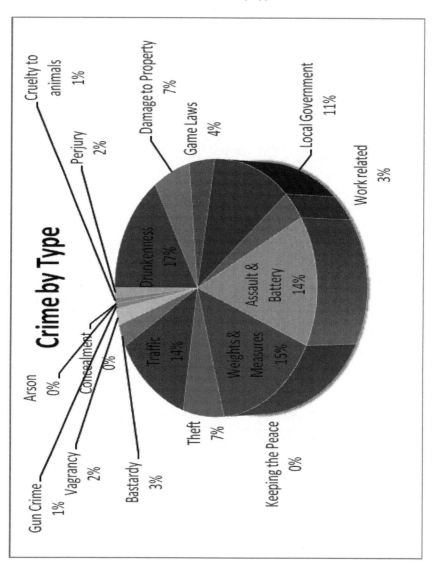

Assault cases account for 14% but they are no longer the most common type of offence ; that position is now taken by Drunkenness at 17%. There were only 5 cases of Game Law offences and 8 cases of Theft. We do however see a dramatic increase in cases relating to Weights and Measures.

Not all cases resulted in guilty verdicts. The actual outcomes of the year's cases are shown

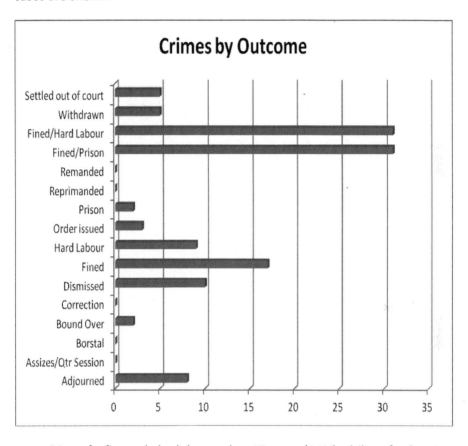

Imposition of a fine only had dropped to 17 cases (14%) whilst a further 62 (50%) cases were given a fine which if not paid would result in imprisonment with or without hard labour.

The details of the fines continued to show a breakdown into the components:

- The value of any costs to witnesses / the constable

- A punitive fine to deter a repeat offence

The value of any damage done to a victim's property is rarely recorded.

The cases where a sentence of 'Fine or Prison' is recorded in the Court Minutes are generally still not formally resolved. It's only if they are recorded in the gaol database that we know they failed to pay the fine.

The court records show that no cases were escalated to the Quarter Session/Assizes.

The gaol database does show records relating to 10 of the 123 cases.

Gaol Record Detail For: John Draper

Record ID:	157
Commital Year:	1871
Reference Doc:	BLARS QGV10/4
ID in Reference Doc:	178
Age:	23
Gender:	male
Height:	5 feet 4½ inches
Hair Colour:	Brown
Eye Colour:	Grey
Complexion:	pale
Visage:	Long
Identifying Features:	Crippled in left hand
Occupation:	Shoemaker
Education:	Imp
Form of Religion:	Church of England
Marital Status:	Single
Birth Town:	Bolnhurst
Birth County:	Bedfordshire
Birth Country:	England
Residence(town/village):	London
Residence(country):	England
Offence:	Burglariously breaking and entering the dwelling house of one Isaac Harlow and stealing therein two coats, one hat, one concertina and other articles at Ravensden on the 16th Feb 1871
When Committed:	18/02/1871
Trial/Conviction Date:	13/03/1871
Trial Type:	Beds Lent Assizes
Trial Verdict:	Guilty
Type of Gaol:	Bedford County Gaol
Sentence:	7 Years Penal Servitude
No. of Previous Convictions:	3
Previous Conviction Details:	Bedford, 1864 Apr 1, House Breaking, Acquitted on Remand. 1864 June 27, Obtaining Goods by False Pretences, 2 Calendar Months. 1867 Beds Mich Sess. Stealing Leather, 18 Calendar Months.
How Disposed:	Removed to Pentonville
Discharge Date:	13/07/1872

The case of John Draper, born in Bolnhurst, is not included in our court records because the crime of theft was committed in Bedford Division. John was convicted of house breaking and theft.

He had a string of previous convictions and was sentenced to 7 years penal servitude (the severe sentence which replaced transportation).

Discharge notes show he was transferred to Pentonville prison.

The database also shows an entry for Thomas Perkins, born in Harrold. He again appeared at the Bedford Division court and was sentenced to 10 days in the Debtors cell.

Of the 10 cases from Bletsoe Division seen in the gaol database the first case in February was for Cruelty to Animals. Joseph Ekins, aged 20, was charged with beating and torturing a pig at Keysoe and after being found guilty was sentenced to 2 months hard labour. He had no previous convictions.

In March we see George Pettit, aged 31, convicted of assault on Mary Ann Hensman at Harrold. George had a previous conviction of 3 weeks hard labour for a Game Law offence in 1868. This time he paid the fine of £1 14s rather than go to prison.

In March there was a case of vagrancy against James Thompson. You will recall there had been a clamp down on vagrants in 1869 when there were five –fold as many cases as normal. James was caught begging in Keysoe by PC Sturgess and was sentenced to 2 weeks in prison.

PC Sturgess had been the arresting officer in the case of the murder of Sarah Marshall by William Bull in Little Staughton in 1870. Bull was executed at Bedford Gaol in April 1871.

Another case of begging, this time at Odell, was heard in June when Thomas Pendred was found guilty of vagrancy and sentenced to 7 days hard labour. In October we see the re-appearance of James Thompson; this time he is begging in Odell and gets 3 weeks hard labour. There is no doubt that a government or county initiative which targets a certain type of crime does result in more cases and hence influences the statistics on patterns of crime.

Later in the year John Pack, a juvenile, was convicted of stealing money from the missionary box at Pertenhall Moravian Chapel. He was convicted to 3 weeks had labour then 4 years in the Reformatory. Theft was also the offence committed by William Crouch at Harrold. He was convicted of stealing 2 eels, value 1s 6d and was sentenced to 3 weeks hard labour.

Another who chose to pay the fine rather than spend 3 months in prison was William Eaton of Farndish. He was convicted of failing to support his wife or his parent (records differ) and was required to pay the arrears to the Wellingborough Union.

The last case of the year saw the accused, Joseph Farrar, aged 30, from Wymington accused of stealing a horse rug, value 10s. He was sentenced to 2 weeks hard labour.

Did the cases held in Bletsoe Petty Session get into the local press? The answer is again definitely YES. It is this decade which sees the highest level of reporting since 104 of the cases (85%) were covered in the local newspaper. Again many of the reports just summarised the case by describing the defendant, the nature of the offence and the outcome. However in a few cases the reports continue to include a very full description of the offence, any items stolen or damaged, the witness statements and the social background of the victim, the defendant and their family.

The article about John Pack gives more detail of how he broke into two missionary boxes at the church on two separate occasions in the same week.

One series of crimes classified as Traffic is detailed in the May newspapers; a group of labourers from Poddington were charged with obstructing the highway and another group charged with laying a timber across the road. George Meadows was common to both groups .George was given a fine or 7 days hard labour for the first charge and a fine or 14 days hard labour for the second charge. He does not appear in the gaol database hence it suggests he paid both fines. All other members of the group except Joseph Brown received similar sentences. Brown's case was recorded as being dismissed though insufficient evidence but, interestingly, Brown had not been listed in the court records.

In June, Thomas Brightman, who had been the subject of an arson attack, was himself the defendant in a new type of case. The police had in the last decade taken over the responsibility of inspections under the Contagious Diseases Act and Brightman was accused of having a flock of sheep affected with Scab and neglecting to inform the police authorities. The newspaper included details of the conflicting veterinary examinations, the failure of witnesses to attend court on multiple occasions and attempts to settle out of court. Overall the magistrates thought the police were quite deficient and therefore concluded the case should be dismissed.

The sequence of events leading to the building of the police station/court was also detailed in the newspapers. The cooperation of John Gibbard in agreeing how to transfer the land in Sharnbrook was particularly noted as were the nature of minor changes to the plans previously prepared by John Horsford. Progress was being made and the tender was published. All results of the tender were detailed in the July 4th newspaper and approval for the go –ahead was being sought from the Secretary of State. The only new hurdle was the illness of John Gibbard.

Sometimes the newpaper articles appear to introduce or reinforce inconstistencies. The case in July where Leo Spencer of Sharnbrook is accused of assaulting Edwin Day, a fishmonger from Bedford is a good example. The court and newspaper accounts are consistent but neither of their names is present in the 1871 census. Leo was sentenced to a fine or 2 months hard labour. There is no record for him in the gaol database.

Who had brought the case against the defendants?

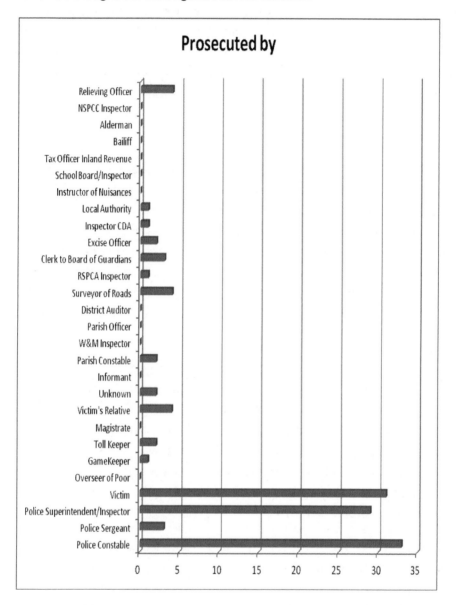

The number of cases prosecuted by the Victim has fallen dramatically to 31 (25%) whilst the proportion of case brought by a police officer increased significantly to 53%. Perhaps surprisingly the role of gamekeeper only accounts for one single case. There are two prosecutions by a Parish

Constable. We do see an increase in the number of different roles named as the plaintiff; many of these new roles are inspectors with specific responsibilities for areas of community health/welfare.

The annual inspections by the HMIC are now a routine event. The report for 1871 shows the strength of the force as 94 i.e. 1 chief constable, 1 clerk, 1 deputy chief constable, 6 superintendents,2 Inspectors, 8 serjeants and 75 constables. The report shows that there are now different classes and pay scales for Superintendents and Serjeants as well as constables. The retirement of Captain Boultbee after 31 years was noted as was the progress in building the police station /court at Sharnbrook. When completed this would mean that 'none of the petty sessional business in the county will be carried out at a public house'.

The withdrawal of licences of Beer Houses in Luton has led to a significant decrease in crime. The magistrate has reported that 'Of the known 300 criminals , 100 have gone to honest employment, 50 have left the neighbourhood and many are now not living on the proceeds of crime. Overall the force was again described as efficient.

This particular year has zero cases in the court records escalated to the Quarter Sessions. Apart from some vagrancy cases all of the 10 cases also seen in the Gaol database were reported in the local newspaper.

Let's again move forward.

References:

(1) Prison Act, 1865 (28 & 29 Vict. c126)

Chapter Seven: 1881

This last decade has seen great changes in Education as major acts set ever increasing levels of compulsory schooling. By 1880 the schooling age had been extended to 10 year olds.

Trade Union Act 1871 was an Act of the Parliament of the United Kingdom which legalised trade unions for the first time in the United Kingdom (1).

The Ballot Act 1872 was an Act of the Parliament of the United Kingdom that introduced the requirement that parliamentary and local government elections in the United Kingdom be held by secret ballot (2). This prevented undue influence from landowners or employers. This had been one of the key Chartists goals.

The Licensing Act of 1872: (3)

- restricted the closing times in public houses to midnight in towns and 11 o'clock in country areas.

- regulated the content of beer. One of the most common practices was to add salt to the beer, which increased the thirst and therefore sales as well.

- said that licensing hours were to be determined by local authorities.

- gave boroughs the option of becoming completely 'dry' i.e. banning all alcohol.

The Public Health Act of 1875 (4) was to combat filthy urban living conditions, which caused various public health threats, including the spread of many diseases such as cholera and typhus. Reformers wanted to resolve sanitary problems, because sewage was flowing down the street daily, including the presence of sewage in living quarters. The Act required all new residential construction to include running water and an internal drainage system. This Act also led to the government prohibiting the construction of shoddy housing by building contractors. The Act also meant that every public health authority had to have a medical officer and a sanitary inspector, to ensure the laws on food, housing, water and hygiene were carried out.

There were only two prime ministers in the decade, Gladstone and Disraeli.

Worldwide there was an economic depression but the UK was able to insulate itself from the worst effects of the financial crisis.

Nationally, the process of taking photographs of prisoners, particularly repeat offenders, was introduced in 1871.

The governments' control of Prisons was reinforced and the use of stocks was discontinued.

In Bedfordshire the Chief Constable was now Lieutenant- Colonel Frederick John Josselyn. The long serving Superintendent Graham retired in 1881 after nearly 40 years as a senior officer in the Bletsoe and Bedford Divisions.

Locally, James Carruthers was still Superintendent at Bletsoe however the opening of the new Police Station and Court in 1872 coincided with a renaming of both the Police Division and the Petty Session Division. Both were now called Sharnbrook rather than Bletsoe.

In 1875 the concerns over costs of maintaining a rural constabulary were again highlighted because Bedfordshire was reported as the most expensive force in the country. Eventually the concerns were quelled because they realised that the 1873 accounts had been abnormally high because of the delayed building of the Sharnbrook Police Station and the extra costs required to meet the pension of the long serving Chief Constable .

James Carruthers is still attending petty session cases throughout the year although one Constabulary personnel record shows Superintendent Kennedy appointed in September 1881.

The fifth of the national censuses was held on the 3rd April 1881 and Sharnbrook's registrar was GC Newell and the enumerator was again a school teacher, John Peters Richards. The census return on 178 schedules showed 830 residents, a decrease of 2% from the 1871 survey. The gender distribution was 425 males and unusually less females at 405; remaining at a consistent level, 293 (35%) were under the age of 14. Sharnbrook was back to being the third most populated village in North Beds. Keysoe's population had decreased by 170 since 1871. The highest population was still in Harrold but like Sharnbrook its population was still falling. In fact some 88% of the villages were experiencing a decrease in population since 1871.

The 1881 total population across all the villages covered by the Bletsoe Division was significantly decreased to 13,406, down by 7%.

Using the 1885 trade directory the Sharnbrook tradesmen now included one postmaster, two bakers, three Blacksmiths, three boot makers, two butchers, a saddler, a draper, a tailor, two carpenters, three plumbers, two millers, a carrier, two builders, three farmers, a watchmaker, three coal merchants, a wheelwright and two surgeons. There were also two publicans and a beer retailer, two builders, a vicar, a station master and a school teacher.

In addition the census showed only 36 agricultural labourers (a decline of over 100 when compared to 1871). There were only 39 skilled agricultural occupations which again is a decline from 1871 hence re-classsification was not the reason for the step change in Aglab numbers. This phenomenon was the subject of a separate study which attempted to determine the fate or whereabouts of the individual 1871 Aglabs.

The numbers of residents employed in domestic service only fell slightly to 89.

During the entirety of 1881 the Petty Sessions were held by one or more of 9 magistrates

Lord St John	HH Green	RRB Orlebar	HR Magniac
Magennis	L Stileman-Gibbard	J Martyn	ES Watson
T Bagnall			

According to the Petty Session Minutes the most cases were heard by Henry Green (85) with Edward Watson next on 45 cases. The fewest number of cases was heard by RRB Orlebar .

The cases were distributed across the year

Jan - Mar	Apr- Jun	Jul- Sep	Oct - Dec	Total
31	58	21	44	154

The highest number of cases in any one session was 21, slightly down on 1871 but still the second highest in the years studied to date.

The number of cases in 1881 classified by type

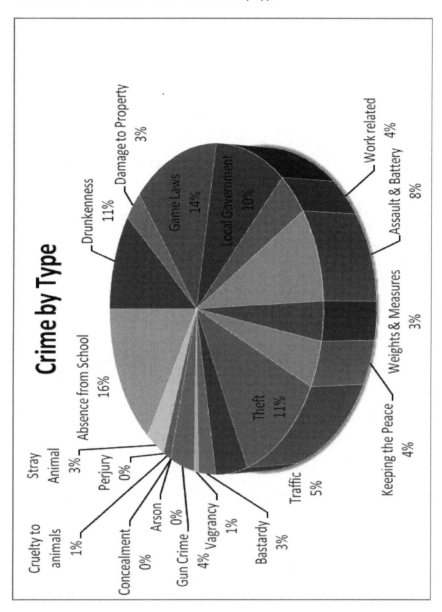

Assault cases now only account for 8% and again but they are not the most common type of offence ; that position is now taken by Absence from School at 16%. These are cases where one or both parents are accused of not sending their child or children to to the local school. Surely this is another example of an initiative resulting in an increased statistic.

Poaching is still quite high accounting for 14% of cases. Asssociated with this is the increased number of cases concerning the use of a gun without a licence.

Drunkenness is slightly reduced and seems to have passed its peak. We do however see a dramatic increase in cases relating to stray animals, normally horses but occassionally cows.The number of cases regarding Weights and Measures has significantly decreased.

 Not all cases resulted in guilty verdicts. The actual outcomes of the year's cases are shown

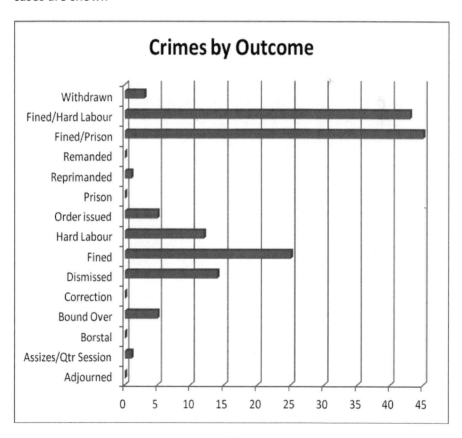

Imposition of a fine only had dropped to 25 cases (16%) whilst a further 88 (57%) cases were given a fine which if not paid would result in imprisonment with or without hard labour.

The details of the fines continue to show a breakdown into the usual components:

- The value of any costs to witnesses / the constable

- A punitive fine to deter a repeat offence

The value of any damage done to a victim's property is again rarely recorded.

The cases where a sentence of 'Fine or Prison' is recorded in the Court Minutes are generally still not formally resolved. It's only if they are recorded in the gaol database that we know they failed to pay the fine.

The court records show that one case was escalated to the Quarter Session/ Assizes. That case was in October against Benjamin Jefferies for stealing a carriage whip values 6s at Bletsoe. The QSR archive shows he received bail for £20 and the case did not get heard until the Epiphany 1882 Quarter Session where there were three witnesses appearing for the prosecution. The indictment record shows 'No true bill' hence the case did not go to the jury.

The gaol database does however show records relating to 16 of the 154 cases.

The case of Josiah Underwood, born in Yardley Hastings, is in both the court records and the gaol database. The 1881 conviction seems to relate to two separate trespasses on Pickering and Lovell land on the same night. The records show two convictions

- 1 month with hard labour

- a fine or 1 calendar month hard labour.

Josiah was one of three men arrested for trespass at the time. The other two men, James White and George King, do not appear in the gaol database.

The gaol record showed the fine was paid and he was discharged after 1 month. Further study of the gaol records showed this was not his first court appearance. He had been convicted of game law offences in late 1880 and again had received a fine or 1 calendar month hard labour. Later in this decade whilst he is still in his thirties he will be convicted of Night Poaching and Poaching for which he received sentences of 3 months hard labour and 1 month hard labour respectively. The gaol database shows that he was not the only Underwood from Yardley Hastings to be convicted of Night Poaching in 1886, a John Underwood, age 25, received a sentence of 12 months hard labour. From the census data, this is most likely Josiah's younger brother, Jonathan.

The database also shows an entry for John Hill born in Hereford. He first appeared at the Sharnbrook Division court in March accused of vagrancy. In the gaol database he is first sentenced to 7 days hard labour and later in the year to 14 days hard labour for a repeat offence.

The case against Alfred Robinson of Harrold was one of a series which saw him spend several spells in Bedford Gaol. The cases were nearly all for Assault including the one in 1881. The gaol database shows he has 4 previous convictions at age 25.

Total records found 10 : Page 1 of 1

	First Name	Last Name	Age	Committal Year	Residence(town/village)	Birth Town	Offence	Sentence	
Detail	Alfred	Robinson	19	1875			Assault	7 Days Hard Labour	
Detail	Alfred	Robinson	20	1876			Assault	2 Calendar Months Hard Labour	
Detail	Alfred	Robinson	22	1878			Disorderly Person	2 Calendar Months Hard Labour or 51/6.	
Detail	Alfred	Robinson	24	1879	Harrold		Assault	2 calendar months hard labour	
Detail	Alfred	Robinson	25	1881	Harrold		Assault	2 calendar months hard labour	
Detail	Alfred	Robinson	29	1884	Harrold		Game Laws	1 calendar month hard labour or 32/6d	
Detail	Alfred	Robinson	30	1884	Harrold		1. Disorderly 2. Assaulting Police Constable	1. 1 calendar month hard labour or 57/2d 2. 2 calendar months hard labour	
Detail	Alfred Vaughan	Robinson	22	1886	Northampton		Perjury	6 Calendar Months Hard Labour	
Detail	Alfred	Robinson	39	1882	Harrold		Assault	2 calendar months hard labour	
Detail	Alfred	Robinson	42	1894	Harrold		Drunkenness	1 calendar month hard labour	

Back To Top

The census shows Alfred is an Aglab living in the High Street, Harrold and is married to Mary with 3 children.

Another case where the outcome was 14 days hard labour was against John Cox from Worcester who was convicted of theft ('stealing a slop, value 2s') at Wymington. John, a 32 year old labourer, had a previous conviction in Northamptonshire.

In June two men were charged with using a gun without a licence at Melchbourne and one of them, Thomas Harris was also accused of assault on the gamekeeper. Thomas, a riveter, had one previous Game Law conviction in 1880 and was born in Rushden. He was sentenced to a fine or 1 month hard labour for the gun crime and a further 1 month hard labour for the assault.

In November Thomas Bates elected to be tried summarily and pleaded guilty to a charge of stealing a shirt and 15 pairs of socks at Wymington. Thomas, a 36 year old stoker born in Lancashire, was sentenced to 1 month hard labour.

The next two cases were both charges of Assault. First, one Joseph Timms of Wymington was convicted of assaulting his wife Sabina and , in his absence, he was sentenced to 6 month hard labour and the judge granted judicial separation i.e. a court order similar to divorce, under which the couple remains legally married but their normal marital obligations cease and they no longer have to go on living together. The gaol database shows his time in Bedford prison didn't start until 1889 and he was discharged in March 1890. The only Sabina Timms in the 1881 census shows she may well have moved back to Buckinghamshire to live with her father in Waddesdon.

The second case of assault was John Savage who was charged with assaulting William Herbert, a bailiff at Harrold. The case was dismissed.

A few days later an additional session was held to hear the charge against George Goodes. He elected to be tried summarily and pleaded guilty to stealing fowl at Little Staughton, value 7s6d. He was sentenced to 6 weeks hard labour. According to the census George was aged 29 and living in Colmworth with his wife Mary; he was a farm labourer. Like so many local women she was a lace maker. A general search for 'lace makers' in

Bedfordshire in 1881 shows 4900 people who have declared that as their profession.

A more severe sentence of 6 months hard labour was given to Samuel Cockings. In 1882 he was convicted of stealing pigeons at Pavenham. The

Gaol Record Detail For: Samuel Cockings

Record ID:	41469
Commital Year:	1882
Reference Doc:	BLARS PRIS2/2/3
ID in Reference Doc:	2927
Age:	28
Gender:	Male
Height:	5 feet 2¾ inches
Hair Colour:	Dark Brown
Occupation:	Labourer
Education:	Imperfect
Form of Religion:	E
Birth Town:	Pavenham
Birth County:	Bedfordshire
Offence:	Stealing pigeons
When Committed:	19/03/1882
Type of Gaol:	Bedford Gaol
Sentence:	6 calendar months hard labour
Discharge Date:	16/09/1882

sentence was perhaps more severe because in 1881 he had a previous conviction for trespass on Pacey land in Sharnbrook . For that he had already been fined quite heavily but since he did not appear in the gaol database we can assume he managed to pay the £2 fine and the 12s6d costs.

He did not again appear in the court records. The census shows he may well have taken his wife Mary and moved to the Bristol area where he started his family. In 1901 he was in Dover employed as a navvy labourer and by 1911 he was a Coble Oven labourer working in Chesterfield, Derbyshire.

In December, George Dickens, a gamekeeper, prosecuted three men for trespass in search of game at Riseley. George Perkins, George Ponton and Thomas Harris were fined 15s, £1 and £2 respectively and given an unspecifid period of hard labour if they did not pay the fine plus costs. The gaol database shows that George Perkins , a shoemaker from Bozeat aged 39, served 1 month hard labour presumably being the only one unable to pay his fine. He had 2 previous convictions in Northamptonshire and went on to commit other game law offences over the next 4 years.

Also in December we see James Prigmore convicted of assault on two women in Felmersham. He was sentenced to 14 days hard labour with another 14 days hard labour to follow on the first imprisonment. One of the women was Lydia, a lace maker, his wife and mother of his 6 sons and 1 daughter. The other woman, Ann Circuit, aged 76, is another lace maker living in Felmersham.

The last 3 cases of this session were complicated because one man, Edward Richardson, aged 14 from Poddington, was prosecuted by two different victims for stealing fowl. Another man, Thomas Brown, aged 13, also from Poddington, was also charged with one of these offences. In the court records Richardson pleaded guilty to one case but this was later dismissed whist he and Brown were convicted to 10 days hard labour and then 5 years at the Reformatory by the Quarter Session hearing.

The last case of the year saw the accused, Thomas Bailey, accused of drunkenness on the Highway. He was sentenced to a fine of 1s plus costs or 3 weeks hard labour. He does not appear in the gaol database.

Did the cases held in Bletsoe Petty Session get into the local press? The answer is again definitely YES. It is this decade which sees the second highest level of reporting since 123 of the cases (80%) were covered in the local newspaper. Again many of the reports just summarised the case by describing the defendant, the nature of the offence and the outcome. However in a few cases the reports continued to include a very full description of the offence, any items stolen or damaged, the witness statements and the social background of the defendant and their family.

In one case against 3 defendants from Sharnbrook we see responsible localbusiness men charged and convicted of stealing watercress from John Gibbard's parkland.

SHARNBROOK.

PETTY SESSIONS.—FRIDAY, MAY 13.
Present: Mr. L. G. S. Gibbard and Mr. E. S. Watson.
Robert Hayes, miller, *James Goff*, blacksmith, and *Richard Bayes*, carter, all of Sharnbrook, were charged with stealing watercress growing in a pond in Mr. Gibbard's park, on the 1st inst. The case was proved by Thomas Pacey, gamekeeper. Fined 1s. and 8s. 6d. costs each.

The article shows they were fined but the court records show they would have served 3 days hard labour if they failed to pay the fine. The census records show Robert Hay to be a corn miller married to Maria with 5 children living on Kennel Hill. James Gough also lived on Kennel Hill with his wife Jane and 2 children. Richard Bayes, at aged 22, was the youngest and lived with his parents on Kennel Hill. None of them appear in the gaol database.

Who had brought the case against the defendants?

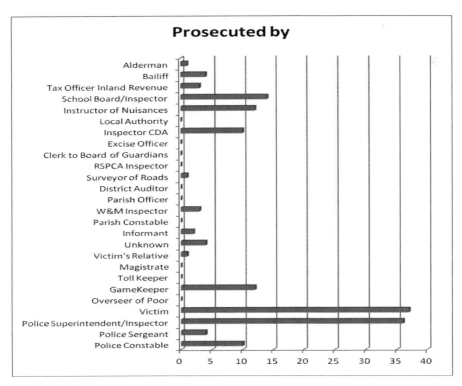

The number of cases prosecuted by the Victim was still the highest at 37 (24%) whilst the proportion of cases brought by a police officer, excluding those where the Superintendent was himself the Weights & Measures or Contagious Diseases Inspector, has decreased to 32%. The role of game keeper /bailiff now accounts for 16 cases (10%).

There are again no prosecutions by a Parish Constable. We do see an increase in the number of different roles named as the plaintiff; many of these new roles are inspectors with specific responsibilities for areas of community health/welfare and schooling.

The annual inspections by the HMIC continue to be a routine event. The report for 1881 shows the strength of the force as 91 i.e. 1 chief constable, 1 clerk, 1 deputy chief constable, 5 superintendents, 2 Inspectors, 9 serjeants and 72 constables. The report lists the extra duties carried out by senior officers

Extra Duties.—The superintendents are inspectors of weights and measures, and under the "Adulteration of Food and Drugs" and "Explosives" Acts; two members of the force act as assistant relieving officers for vagrants, and 18 assist the chief constable, when necessary, under the "Contagious Diseases (Animals) Act;" the police keep order in and about the courts of assize.

There had been a considerable increase in indictable offences compared to the previous year but drunkenness had continued to decline.

Crime.—

YEARS.	Indictable Offences.		Offences Determined Summarily.		Drunkenness and Drunk and Disorderly.		Assaults on Police.	
	Reported to the Police.	Number of Persons Apprehended for the same.	Number of Persons Proceeded against.	Number of Persons Convicted.	Number of Persons Proceeded against.	Number of Persons Convicted.	Number of Persons Proceeded against.	Number of Persons Convicted.
	1.	2.	3.	4.	5.	6.	7.	8.
1880 - - -	72	76	1,270	1,146	206	199	11	10
1881 - - -	102	61	1,281	1,143	176	168	14	13

Note.—Columns 5, 6, 7, and 8 included in Columns 2, 3, and 4.

For the first time there was no adverse comment about the lack of court / gaol facilities in the Bletsoe/Sharnbrook Division. The overall conclusion was the County force was operating efficiently.

Let's again move forward.

References:

(1) Trade Union Act 1871 (34 & 35 Vict c 31)

(2) Ballot Act 1872 (35 & 36 Vict. c. 33)

(3) Licensing Act 1872 (35 & 36 Vict c. 94)

(4) Public Health Act (38 & 39 c 55)

Chapter Eight: 1891

The Corrupt and Illegal Practices Prevention Act was an Act of the Parliament of the United Kingdom of Great Britain and Ireland in 1883 (1). It was a continuation of policy to make voters free from the intimidation of landowners and politicians. It criminalised attempts to bribe voters and standardised the amount that could be spent on election expenses.

The Representation of the People Act (2) known informally as the Third Reform Act and the Redistribution Act (3) of the following year were laws which further extended the suffrage in Britain and included the vote for agricultural workers. These measures extended the same voting qualifications as existed in the towns to the countryside, and essentially established the modern one member constituency as the normal pattern for Parliamentary representation.

The recently appointed Chief Secretary of Ireland, Lord Frederick Cavendish, and his under-secretary TH Burke were stabbed to death in 1882 in Phoenix Park, Dublin. The perpetrators were members of the 'Invincibles', an extremist branch of the 'Fenian' revolutionary organisation. The murders outraged the public in Britain and, much against his will, provoked Prime Minister Gladstone into maintaining harsh coercive policies in Ireland. The Chief Secretary was married to Lucy Cavendish, the niece of the Prime Minister William Ewart Gladstone.

Under the 1888 Local Government Act, passed by the Conservatives, responsibility for poor law relief, roads, bridges and asylum was transferred to newly-created county councils. Even policing was now controlled by a Standing Joint Committee (SJC) – this reported to the County Council but it still retained a membership based mainly on the Quarter Session Magistrates.

This year also saw the demotion of the senior role in the Sharnbrook Division from Superintendent to Inspector. Sharnbrook was by far the smallest and quietest of the Divisions and its eventual absorption into an enlarged Bedford Division had begun.

In London the end of this decade has seen the 'Jack the Ripper' murders. The last of the so called "Whitechapel" murders is discovered with the death in Castle Alley on 17 July 1889 of Alice McKenzie a.k.a. "Clay Pipe" Alice.

There were only two prime ministers in the decade, Gladstone and Robert

Arthur Talbot Gascoyne-Cecil, **3rd Marquess of Salisbury.** He served as a Conservative PM in 1885-86 and again in 1886-92. He was the last Prime Minister to head his full administration from the House of Lords.

Worldwide, the Long Depression continued for all of the decade and UK profits and growth both diminished.

Locally, Henry Quenby was the Superintendent who was demoted to Inspector. After a few years the pain was reduced as he goes to Bedford Division as Deputy Chief Constable. Inspector Ebeneezer Cain joins Sharnbrook Division and immediately conducts an audit of the Police Station facilities.

The sixth of the national censuses was held on the 5th April 1891 and Sharnbrook's registrar was again George C Newell from Milton Ernest and the enumerator was his son, Edward Furnivall Newell, a local master baker. The census return on 184 schedules showed only 761 residents, a decrease of 8% from the 1881 survey. The gender distribution was 350 males and 411 females; 236 (31%) were under the age of 14.

Using the 1890 trade directory the Sharnbrook tradesmen now included one postmaster, two bakers, two Blacksmiths, three boot makers, two butchers, a saddler, a draper, a tailor, two carpenters, three plumbers, two millers, two carriers, five farmers or bailiffs, a watchmaker, four coal merchants, a wheelwright, two brick makers, one bricklayer and two surgeons. There were also two publicans and a beer retailer, a vicar, a station master and a school teacher. The directory named a Deputy Registrar of Births, Marriages and Deaths as John Newell and census data shows he was another baker and brother to George, the registrar.

In addition the census showed only 52 agricultural labourers (a small increase when compared to 1881). There were only 21 skilled agricultural occupations which again is a decline from 1881 and since the combined numbers are identical to 1881 it suggested this is just re-classsification of occupations. Certainly there had been no return to the Aglab numbers seen in 1871. The numbers of residents employed in domestic service only remained constant.

During the entirety of 1891 the Petty Sessions were held by one or more of 9 magistrates.

Lord St John	AD Chapman	RRB Orlebar	Capt JCR Scott
Green	L Stileman-Gibbard	Wilkinson	Browning
RC Alston			

According to the Petty Session Minutes the most cases were heard by Richard Orlebar (38) with Chapman next on 33 cases. The fewest number of cases was heard by Rowland Alston.

The cases were distributed across the year

Jan - Mar	Apr- Jun	Jul- Sep	Oct - Dec	Total
25	21	19	48	113

This is considerably less than seen in 1881. The decrease is around 27% and this is the smallest number seen so far in any one year . The highest number of cases in any one session was only 13, well down on 1881, and again is the lowest number seen so far.

The number of cases in 1891 classified by type

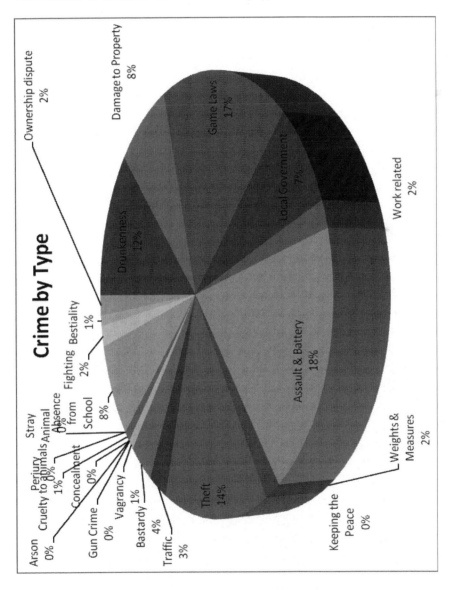

Crime by Type

- Ownership dispute 2%
- Damage to Property 8%
- Game Laws 17%
- Local Government 7%
- Work related 2%
- Drunkenness 12%
- Bestiality 1%
- Fighting 2%
- Absence from School 8%
- Stray Animal 0%
- Cruelty to animals 1%
- Periury 0%
- Concealment 0%
- Arson 0%
- Gun Crime 0%
- Vagrancy 0%
- Bastardy 1%
- Traffic 4%
- Theft 14%
- Assault & Battery 18%
- Weights & Measures 2%
- Keeping the Peace 0%

Assault cases now account for 18% and they are the most common type of offence. Poaching and Game Law offences come a close second at 17% although there are no instances of cases of gun crime. Absence from School has fallen to only 8%. Drunkenness and Theft have remained fairly constant around 12%.The number of cases regarding Weights and Measures has significantly decreased to less than 2%.

 Not all cases resulted in guilty verdicts. The actual outcomes of the year's cases are shown

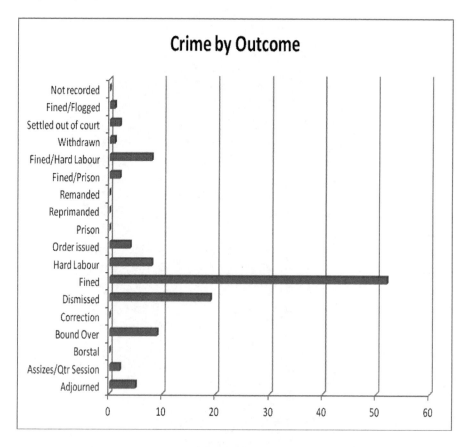

Imposition of only a fine had significantly increased to 52 cases (46%) whilst only a further 10 (9%) cases were given a fine which if not paid would result in imprisonment with or without hard labour.

The details of the fines continued to show a breakdown into the two usual components:

- The value of any costs to witnesses / the constable

- A punitive fine to deter a repeat offence

The value of any damage done to a victim's property was rarely recorded. The case records started to indicate how much time a defendant had to raise the money to pay the fine.

The cases where a sentence of 'Fine or Prison' was recorded in the Court Minutes are generally still not formally resolved. It's only if they are recorded in the gaol database that we know they failed to pay the fine.

The number of cases dismissed reaches a new peak at 17%.

The court records showed that two cases were escalated to the Quarter Session/ Assizes. The first case was in May against Samuel Watson for stealing a sheep value £3 at Knotting. The QSR archive, QSR1891/3/5/3, showed a complex series of offences : 1st count - stealing 1 ewe; 2nd count - stealing 1 sheep; 3rd count - stealing 8lbs of mutton; 4th count - killing 1 ewe with intent to steal a part of the carcass; 5th count - killing 1 sheep with intent to steal a part of the carcass. Samuel pleaded Guilty and admitted previous convictions. He was sentenced to 12 calendar months hard labour, one of the most severe sentences we have seen. The gaol database showed Samuel was born in Elsworth, Cambridgeshire and that he had 14 previous convictions. Since there are no other records for him at Bedford Gaol and the 1891 census shows him living in Brook Street, Elsworth we must assume he was a repeat offender in Cambridgeshire.

The second case was a charge against George Neal, aged 23, an Aglab living in Riseley, for having unlawful connection with a cow. The case does not appear in the Quarter Session records but the gaol database confirms he served a 6 month hard labour sentence in Bedford. He had no previous convictions.

In addition to these cases the gaol database showed another 11 records relating to the 113 cases in the year.

At the first session of the year there were two cases of Poaching. Both men, George Cartwright and William Stanley were convicted and sentenced to a fine of £1 and 11s costs or 1 month imprisonment. Cartwright was also required to have his gun destroyed. The gaol record shows he was a bricklayer born in Kimbolton and served his sentence in Bedford. The census record shows he was head of a family with 7 children living in Flanders Yard, Irchester. William was a shoe maker born in Little Harrowden but also living in Irchester . He was also discharged in February. The gaol database records show that both men served their 1 month with hard labour.

In February another 2 men were charged with the same crime but this time they had very different sentences. Herbert Willmott and Herbert Denton were charged with stealing 2 live fowls value 2s. Both were found guilty and Willmott was sentenced to a fine of £1 plus £ 4s/6d costs. Denton, on the other hand, had a previous conviction in Northamptonshire and was sentenced to 3 weeks hard labour. The gaol record shows he was only 16 and had been born in Riseley.

Gaol Record Detail For: Charles Ward

Record ID:	46417
Commital Year:	1891
Reference Doc:	BLARS PRIS2/2/5
ID in Reference Doc:	7895
Age:	53
Gender:	Male
Height:	5 feet 3¼ inches
Hair Colour:	Dark Brown
Occupation:	Labourer
Education:	Neither
Form of Religion:	Church of England
Birth Town:	Northampton
Offence:	Vagrancy
When Committed:	01/05/1891
Type of Gaol:	Bedford Gaol
Sentence:	7 days hard labour
No. of Previous Convictions:	5
Discharge Date:	07/05/1891

A sentence of hard labour was also given to Charles Ward for unlawful begging at Riseley.

The gaol record shows he is aged 53 and has 5 previous convictions. He served 7 days hard labour.

Not surprisingly, finding him on the census has been impossible.

In August there was a case against Thomas J Tebbutt Robinson, a labourer in Milton Ernest, for aggravated assault against his wife, Elizabeth. He was sentenced to 2 months Hard Labour and bound over for £20 plus separation order and maintenance and child support. The gaol database shows that he had served 3 weeks hard labour in 1873 for being drunk and riotous. He had also served a 6week hard labour sentence having been found guilty of embezzlement. In fact his last record shows he has had 3 previous convictions.

A heavy fine of £5 with 12s 6d costs or 2 months hard labour was the sentence given to Thomas Loveridge. Thomas had been found guilty of using a snare for taking game at Knotting. He had been prosecuted by the gamekeeper, George Lamb. Thomas was aged 37, a shoe finisher and born in Olney. Finding him on the census proved impossible but the gaol database does show 7 previous convictions and we know he served 2 hard labour sentences in Bedford for game law offences in 1883. There are other Bedford Gaol records for game law offences committed by a Thomas Loveridge but although his stated age is roughly correct the birthplace is given as Chatham. Coincidentally, taking these into account would add to 7 previous convictions.

In October William Coles , aged 27 and a shoe riveter, appeared on two charges, the first was for Night Poaching and the second for assault on a police constable whilst on duty. The PC was Thomas Sturgess who had arrested William Bull, the murderer, back in 1871. William was found guilty on both charges and received two consecutive sentences of 2 months hard labour. In 1893 he was to go on and commit another offence under the Game Laws Act. He was sentenced to 3 calendar months hard labour and required to enter into a recognizance of £10 and two sureties of £5 each or serve 6 calendar months. He found the sureties this time but in 1894 was convicted of stealing a rabbit and served 14 days hard labour in Bedford Gaol.

Ten days later PC Sturgess was in court again and yes he had been assaulted whilst on duty. Oliver Ellis, aged 24, a shoe finisher born in Poddington, was found guilty and sentenced to 3 months hard labour. The census shows Oliver lived alone at Abbots Yard, Higham Ferrers. George Dilley was his co-defendant on the same charge. George was aged 30, a shoemaker born in Shefford. He was also found guilty and served the 3 months hard labour. In 1887 He had been convicted of night poaching and had been sentenced to 3 calendar months and sureties or a further 6 calendar months.

Not all assault cases resulted in outcomes of hard labour. Abner Wildman was prosecuted by Ruth Horner for an assault at Little Staughton. He was found guilty but only received a fine of 10s plus 10s6d costs.

Late in October, two men, Joseph Dilley, aged 18, a labourer born in Clifton, and George Paxton were convicted of damaging a milestone. Neither men appeared at the session but warrants were raised and they were eventually sentenced to 1 month hard Labour or fined 2s/6d plus 14s 3d damage plus 11s 6d costs. Joseph is seen in the gaol database but George's absence indicates he was able to pay the fine.

The last 2 cases of this year were heard on Christmas Eve. Amos Hulatt was found guilty of being drunk and disorderly in Pavenham and was fined 10s plus 8s/6d costs. Samuel Wilmot was convicted of assault on Thomas Birch at Bletsoe and although the case was adjourned, he was later sentenced to 1 month hard labour. He completed his sentence at Bedford Gaol in February 1892.

Did the cases held in Sharnbrook Petty Session get into the local press? The answer is again definitely YES. In this decade the level of reporting court cases fell slightly but we still see that 67% of cases were covered in the local newspaper. Again many of the reports just summarised the case by describing the defendant, the nature of the offence and the outcome. However in a few cases the reports continued to include a very full description of the offence, any items stolen or damaged, the witness statements and the any key factors of the social background of the defendant.

In one case Jabez Law, a labourer from Swineshead was prosecuted by John Brawn, a farmer in Melchbourne, for breach of contract of service. Jabez had failed to complete the rolling of a field and when questioned he admitted he had just walked away. Brawn had to bring the horse up to the field again and it only took 10 minutes to finish the task. Jabez was found guilty and was ordered to pay 12s damages and 6s 6d costs.

Even more detail was given in the report of the prosecution by the RSPCA Inspector Craigen of cruelty to a horse at Riseley. Farmer Henry Campion was charged with ill treating a mare by requiring it to walk from Bletsoe to Kimbolton when it had a lame leg. His defence was that he had asked Arthur Brown, the boy who was with the animal, to stop at intervals hence avoiding any cruelty. The magistrates decided to dismiss the case.

The story relating the scene for the assault on his wife by Thomas Robinson was very graphic. As she made his breakfast at 05:30 in the morning he complained of being stiff and she said it was because he was getting drunk so often and lying on the ground. He stated that he knew who had told her and went upstairs with a shoe and thrashed his children whilst they were in bed. He then threw several things at her hitting her once. He was regularly coming home drunk and had threatened her with a hatchet. She could no longer live with him. He was sentenced to 2 months hard labour and bound over to keep the peace for 6 months. On the application of the wife she was granted a separation order and he was ordered to pay 2s 6d per week towards the support of the children.

The case against Thomas Loveridge is amplified in a September newspaper. George Lamb was the game keeper for the Magniac family and he described how he and Frederick Whittimore were on land in Knotting when they found several snares. They waited and eventually saw Thomas come into the field and collect these and other snares, he had other snares in his pocket. Returning the next day they found up to 20 snares one of which had a hare trapped. The court recognised that he had received several fines of £5 for previous similar offences and this time fined him the same £5 but with 12s6d cost or 2 months hard labour.

Who had brought the case against the defendants?

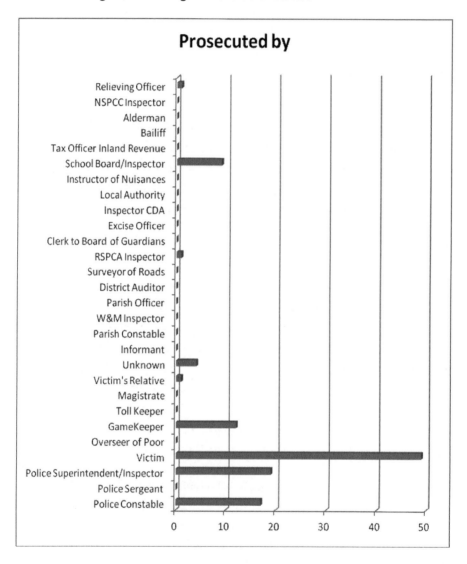

The number of cases prosecuted by the Victim is still the highest at 49 (43%) whilst the proportion of case brought by a police officer, excluding those where the Superintendent is himself the Weights & Measures or Contagious Diseases Inspector, has remained constant at 32%. The role of game keeper /bailiff again accounts for circa 11% of cases. There are again no prosecutions by a Parish Constable and more surprisingly none specifically attributed to the Weights and Measures Inspector. For the first time we do see a decrease in the number of different roles named as the plaintiff; new roles are added but others are no longer active. Overall this is a quiet year and the number of cases is relatively low.

The annual inspections by the HMIC continue to be a routine event. The report for 1891 shows the strength of the force as 96 i.e. 1 chief constable, 1 clerk, 1 deputy chief constable, 4 superintendents, 4 Inspectors, 11 serjeants and 74 constables. The report lists the extra duties carried out by senior officers but notes that they no longer deal with Weights and Measures.

Compared to the previous year there had been a slight decrease in indictable offences but assaults on the police had increased.

Crime.—

YEARS.	Indictable Offences.		Offences Determined Summarily.		Drunkenness and Drunk and Disorderly.		Assaults on Police.	
	Reported to the Police.	Number of Persons Apprehended for the same.	Number of Persons Proceeded against.	Number of Persons Convicted.	Number of Persons Proceeded against.	Number of Persons Convicted.	Number of Persons Proceeded against.	Number of Persons Convicted.
	1.	2.	3.	4.	5.	6.	7.	8.
1890 · · ·	66	27	1,125	1,017	210	200	9	9
1891 · · ·	48	19	1,031	932	187	185	11	11

Note.—Columns 5, 6, 7, and 8 included in Columns 2, 3, and 4.

Overall the force was deemed to be efficient.

Let's again move forward, this time to the 20th Century.

References:

(1) The Corrupt and Illegal Practices Prevention Act 1883 (46 & 47 Vict c. 51)

(2) The Representation of the People Act 1884 (48 & 49 Vict. c. 3)

(3) The Redistribution of Seats Act 1885 (48 & 49 Vict., c. 23)

Chapter Nine: 1901

Local Government changes in 1894 introduced a lower tier of Parish Councils.

A national coal strike sees police from Bedfordshire sent to assist the Derbyshire Rural Police Constabulary. Police constables are required to undertake training in first aid and pass an examination.

In 1896 a regulation enabled the Police to take photographs and measurements of convicted prisoners to aid in future identifications of repeat offenders(1).

The second Boer War starts in 1899 and retired police constables are re-employed to provide cover for those officers volunteering for army service.

Queen Victoria dies in January 1901 and is succeeded by Edward VII.

Worldwide economic depression ended in 1896 and London strengthened its position as the world's financial capital. The export of capital was a major base of the British economy , the "golden era" of international finance.

Gladstone's last period of office as Prime Minister was 1892-94. His Second

Irish Home Rule Bill passed the Commons but was defeated in the Lords in 1893. Gladstone resigned in March 1894, in opposition to increased naval expenditure. He left Parliament in 1895 and died three years later aged 88.

He was succeeded as PM and leader of the Liberal Party by **the Earl of Rosebury**. A year later he lost the 1895 election and the Conservative Marquess of Salisbury started his third term as Prime Minister

The MP for Bedford was again a JP named Samuel Whitbread, this time the eldest son of the Samuel Charles Whitbread who was chairman of the Quarter Sessions in 1839. Charles Pym succeeded him after the election in 1895. In 1896 Pym spoke in Parliament about the continuation of the assizes in Bedford.

In Bedfordshire Josselyn was still Chief Constable but since 1897 Sharnbrook Division had George Daniels as its Inspector. During this current year 1901 he was replaced by John Nottingham. This decade saw the start of co-operation between the County and Bedford and Luton Borough forces. The SJC's willingness to contribute to the Borough officer' pension scheme was pivotal. There were some local riot events where the forces acted together to keep the peace.

The sixth of the national censuses was held on the 31st March 1901 and Sharnbrook's registrar was still George C Newell and the enumerator was again Edward Newell. The description shows that Sharnbrook had started to grow along the Odell Road. The census return on 172 schedules showed 685 residents, a decrease of 10% from the 1891 survey. The gender distribution was308 males and 377 females; the numbers under the age of 14 fell significantly to only 26%. Sharnbrook was still the third most populated village in North Beds. The highest population was still in Harrold but like Sharnbrook its population was still falling. In fact the largest decrease is seen at Riseley, the second largest village. Overall only two villages, Oakley and Wymington, had seen growth in the two recent decades. The population of the North Bedfordshire villages had decreased by 2500 in the last twenty years.

Using the 1903 trade directory the Sharnbrook tradesmen now included one postmaster, one baker, three Blacksmiths, two boot makers, four butchers, a saddler, two drapers, two dress makers, two plumbers, two millers, two carriers, a builder, eight farmers or bailiffs, a watchmaker, four coal merchants and a surgeon. There were also two publicans and a beer retailer, a builder, a vicar, a station master, a brick maker and a school teacher.

In addition the census showed only 17 agricultural labourers (a decline of over 120 when compared to 1871). There were 47 recorded as skilled agricultural workers which is an increase on 1891 hence suggests that re-classsification of occupation does perhaps explain this further decrease in Aglab numbers.

The numbers of residents employed in domestic service fell dramatically by 25%.

During the entirety of 1901 the Petty Sessions were held by one or more of 10 magistrates

HBO Lord St John	Alston	RRB Orlebar	R Orlebar
WC Watson	L Stileman-Gibbard	Capt HE Browning	W Whitworth
FV Dalton	Hipwell	EL Welstead	

According to the Petty Session Minutes by far the most cases were heard by Leonard Gibbard Stileman-Gibbard (71) with Orlebar next on 38 cases (however this could have been any combination of the two Orlebars who were magistrates at this time. The fewest number of cases was heard by William Clarence Watson.

The cases were distributed across the year

Jan - Mar	Apr- Jun	Jul- Sep	Oct - Dec	Total
14	46	22	36	118

The highest number of cases in any one session was 28, the highest number seen to date in what is one of the quietest years in the study period.

The Minutes were now written in a structured format and the information was generally complete. The standard of data recording had slightly improved since all cases did record the nature of the crime and most now recorded where the crime had been committed. An example of the records is shown below.

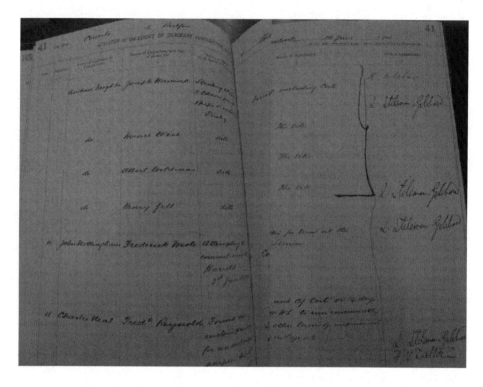

The number of cases in 1901 classified by type

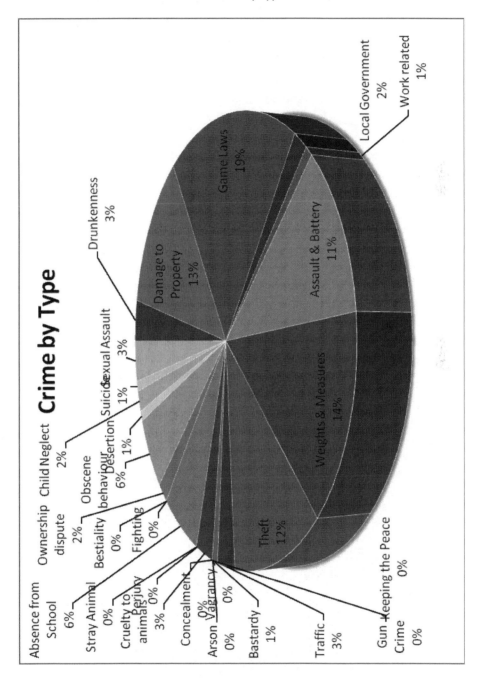

Crime by Type

Game Laws 19%

Local Government 2%

Work related 1%

Drunkenness 3%

Assault & Battery 11%

Damage to Property 13%

Sexual Assault 3%

Suicide 1%

Desertion 1%

Obscene behaviour 6%

Weights & Measures 14%

Child Neglect 2%

Ownership dispute 2%

Bestiality 0%

Fighting 0%

Theft 12%

Absence from School 6%

Stray Animal 0%

Cruelty to animals 3%

Perjury 0%

Concealment 0%

Arson 0%

Vagrancy 0%

Bastardy 1%

Traffic 3%

Keeping the Peace 0%

Gun Crime 0%

Assault cases now only account for 11% and again they are not the most common type of offence ; that position is now taken by Game Law Offences at 19%. This time there are no associated cases of gun crime. Drunkenness is very significantly reduced .Theft has remained at a constant level but damage to property has increased. The number of Weights and Measures cases has returned to its 1871 level . We do see a new crime called Obscene Behaviour which represents 6% of all cases.

Not all cases resulted in guilty verdicts. The actual outcomes of the year's cases are shown

Crime by Outcome

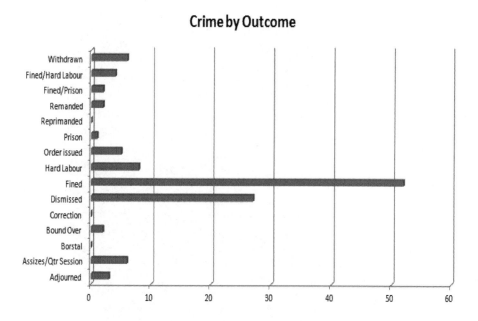

Imposition of a fine only had increased to 52 cases (44%) whilst a further 6 (5%) cases were given a fine which if not paid would result in imprisonment with or without hard labour.

The details of the fines continued to show a breakdown into the usual two components:

- The value of any costs to witnesses / the constable

- A punitive fine to deter a repeat offence

The value of any damage done to a victim's property was rarely recorded.

The cases where a sentence of 'Fine or Prison' is recorded in the Court Minutes were generally still not formally resolved. It's only if they were recorded in the gaol database that we know they failed to pay the fine.

The court records showed that six cases were escalated to the Quarter Session/ Assizes. These included the first and only case of suicide seen during the study period. Frederick Mole from Harrold was accused of unlawfully and wilfully attempting and endeavouring feloniously wilfully and of malice aforethought to kill and murder himself. Gibbard committed him to appear before the next Quarter Session where he pleaded guilty, was sentenced to 6 calendar months imprisonment without hard labour in the 1st division. Witness costs were given to Lucy Bradshaw, leather dresser and wife of Joseph Bradshaw of Harrold, George Javens, Police Constable of Harrold and John French Somerville, surgeon of Harrold. The census shows that John Frederick Mole was aged 43 and lodged with the Crawley family in the High Street. His occupation was as an Upholsterer.Since there are no records dated after 1898 there is no entry for Frederick Mole in the gaol database.

Late in September Henry Slater alias Summerlin from Radwell was charged with stealing a mare and bridle value £35 the property of William Lenton Peck. He was sent to the next Quarter Session on a surety of £5 where he pleaded guilty and was sentenced to 9 months hard labour.

Within a month there were 4 men accused of indecent assaulting Maggie Sabey. The census shows Maggie is a domestic cook working for a retired railway contractor in Bedford. All 4 men were from Thurleigh and they were also sent to the next Quarter Session on a surety of £5. Frederick Holley, Charles Holley, Frank Asplin and William Cowley all pleaded not guilty. Two of them, Charles Holley and Frank Asplin were found Guilty of common assault and each were sentenced to pay a fine of £2 or 1 month imprisonment. The two Holley boys and William Cowley were all Aglabs living at Cross End. Frank was only aged 15 and lived in Keysoe Row.

In June, the defendant Frederick Reynolds faced 3 consecutive charges for stealing fowl, assault and assault on a police officer. His was found guilty of all offences and sentenced to a fined£ 3 plus 12s costs or 14days Hard Labour to run concurrently with 2 other terms of imprisonment of 2 months hard labour and 1 month hard labour.

An unusually high proportion of cases were dismissed during this year. A case of child neglect against Joseph Wagstaff from Colmworth was dismissed by Orlebar and Alston in February. At the same session Wagstaff was charged with Assault on his wife Sarah. This case was withdrawn. Joseph and Sarah appear in the 1891 census with baby son Herbert. In 1901 Joseph, a shepherd, is still living at Mill Cottage with 'Birt' but there is no record for Sarah.

In May, Police Superintendent Nottingham prosecuted Alice Zanker for selling beer and spirits without a licence in Thurleigh. Alice's husband was a publican from Cauldwell Street in Bedford. The case was dismissed on payment of 5s costs.

In June Charles Collyer, a bailiff, prosecuted 6 men for Wilful damage to grassland, value 1s. All 6 cases were dismissed on payment of 5s 10d costs.

The severest sentence during the year was given to Frederick Whitmore for malicious damage to 2 Ash trees at Bolnhurst. He was found guilty and sentenced to 6 months hard labour. The census shows him aged 26 as a member of the single, 104-strong group within Bedford Prison. What is noticeable is that most of the prisoners have their place of birth in the London area.

Four of the first 10 cases in the year were charges of assault. Joseph Wagstaff we have already mentioned.

Arthur Knight was prosecuted by James Chambers for an assault on him at Harrold. He was found guilty and was sentenced to a fine of 10s plus 12s 6d costs or 14 days in prison.

In February, Charles Bardell of Colmworth had been convicted of aggravated assault on his wife Louisa and the court now gave an order for a legal separation. He did not appear before the court hence the case was adjourned. In the March census Charles, a butcher, was still living with Louisa and their 5 children at Church End.

Also in February we saw Alfred Burgess prosecuting Frank Saunderson for an assault at Little Staughton. This case was also dismissed.

The last session of the year saw another appearance by Abner Wildman of Thurleigh. He faced two charges; one for assault on B Catlin and a second for damage to Catlin's bicycle value 6s 6d. The census records shows that Abner was a carpenter and suggest that B Catlin was a Bedford- based bricklayer named Benjamin. Both cases were adjourned for 14 days and then dismissed in 1902.

Did the cases held in Bletsoe Petty Session get into the local press? The answer is again definitely YES. In this decade the level of reporting remains quite high at 92 cases (78%). Again many of the reports just summarised the case by describing the defendant, the nature of the offence and the outcome. However in a few cases the reports continued to include a very full description of the offence, any items stolen or damaged, the witness statements and the social background of the defendant and their family.

The case against Alice Zanker went into great detail describing how she had been challenged by a PC Pedley for not having a licence to sell beer at the Red Lion Public house in Thurleigh. Her defence was that she believed a transfer of licence to her husband had been agreed by the court and that she was acting legally. In fact the licence transfer had been refused even though these transfers were normally very straightforward. The fact that Alice had both pleaded guilty and stopped serving when challenged and had closed the premises was taken into account. This, together with the good reputation of her husband, who had had many years of service as a publican, all contributed to the dismissal of the case recognising that Alice had no idea or intention of evading the Licensing Act.

DISMISSED.

Frank Saunderson, horsekeeper, of Little Staughton, was summoned for assaulting Alfred W. C. Burgess on February 13th, at Little Staughton.—Mr. Clare defended and pleaded not guilty.—Complainant, a farmer, of Colmworth, said he was going along the road from Colmworth to Bushmead, when the defendant came out of a field, which is in the occupation of his father. He asked witness if he had sent a policeman to him, and on being answered in the negative, he used bad language and put his fist in his face. He threatened him but did not strike him.—George Stapleton gave corroborative evidence.—After a lengthy argument between the defendant's solicitor and the Bench as to what constituted an assault the case was dismissed with a caution to the defendant.

The case against Frank Saunderson, described a horsekeeper, was a good example of the problems faced by the magistrates when two men get into an argument and raise their fists. In this case there was no reciprocal accusation but clearly the magistrate didn't think the actions merited a fine or imprisonment. Frank did receive a caution.

The cases against Frederick Reynolds were equally graphic. The report starts by saying that the defendant from Rushden could not remember anything about the events of the case so on advice he pleaded guilty to all three offences. The witnesses gave a detailed account of how 5 men were seen near the hen house at Harrold. The witness got dressed and followed them upon which he was assaulted. When PC Javens arrived and pursued the men to Harrold Wood he also was assaulted by the defendant. Whilst the PC tried to arrest the defendant his friends threw stones at the PC and the witness. The report does not state whether any of the other men were arrested.

The reporter on the case against Thomas Aldridge certainly enjoyed the witness's statement. Thomas, a shoehand from Lavendon, was charged with trespassing in search of game at Harrold. He had failed to appear at the first hearing and an arrest order had been issued. Thomas pleaded not guilty and his defence was to question repeatedly whether the witness's identification of him was sound. William Thorby, a gamekeeper, was adamant that he could identify Thomas as the poacher who ran away. When challenged by the magistrate, the witness said "I know him by his eyelashes as well as by his face and features". The report highlights the fact that there was laughter in the court at this point.

A DRUNKEN FREAK.

Henry Slater, alias Summerlin, labourer, was charged with stealing a grey mare and cart bridle, valued at £35, the property of W. L. Peck.—Prisoner pleaded guilty.—Mr. C. Stimson prosecuted. He said defendant stated that he was drunk at the time and wanted a ride, but when he became sober and found himself at Kempston he was frightened at what he had done and let the horse go.—Prisoner put in a statement to the same effect.—As he had been previously convicted he was sentenced to nine months' hard labour, the Chairman remarking that the plea of drunkenness was of no use.

The report on the case of Henry Slater suggests that the whole thing was not so much a deliberate act of horse stealing but a prank that went wrong because he was drunk. The magistrate was not sympathetic particularly because of previous convictions. Henry had been court-martialled in 1899 for breaking out of Mountjoy Barracks, Dublin and theft for which he served a sentence of 3 months hard labour. He had also been summarily convicted of malicious damage and fraudulent enlistment.

The case against the four men accused of indecent assault at Thurleigh was also amplified in the local newspaper. It seems that the men only tried to kiss her. Witnesses supported the defendants' claims that they did not exceed their own descriptions of the events. The local vicar gave reports of good behaviour for the boys. In finding two of them guilty of common assault only, the magistrate recognised this was their first offence and only imposed a fine of £2. Two men were discharged.

Who had brought the case against the defendants?

Prosecuted by

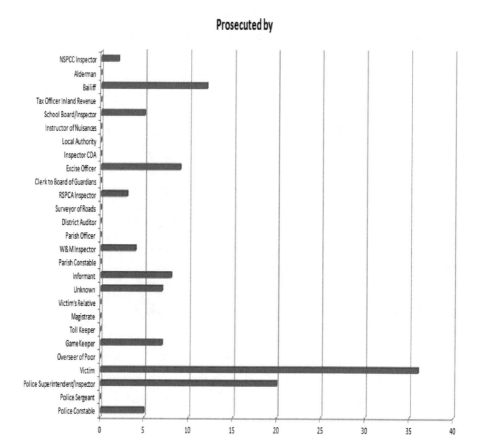

The number of cases prosecuted by the Victim was still the highest at 36 (31%) whilst the proportion of cases brought by a police officer had decreased to 21%. The role of gamekeeper /bailiff now accounted for 19 cases (16%). There was again no prosecutions by a Parish Constable. We did see a larger increase in the number of different roles named as the plaintiff; many of these new roles were inspectors with specific responsibilities for areas of community health/welfare /taxation.

The annual inspections by the HMIC continued to be a routine event. The report for 1901 was not available but the report dated 1900 shows the strength of the force as 99 i.e. 1 chief constable, 1 clerk, 1 deputy chief constable, 4 superintendents, 4 Inspectors, 12 serjeants and 76 constables.

The report listed the extra duties carried out by senior officers and specifically mentions that the Inspector in charge of the Sharnbrook Division had an elevated pay of £120 per annum. All the senior officers were authorised as Inspectors under the Contagious Diseases Act, the Superintendents and the Sharnbrook Inspector was also authorised as Inspectors under the Explosives Act.

79 of the officers held valid certificates from St John's Ambulance Association.

The number of crimes had increased slightly and drunkenness was again on the increase; the overall conclusion of the inspection was that the force was efficient but in this instance it was recorded that they had visited all stations except Sharnbrook.

It's worth noting that the Bedford Borough force had significantly increased its numbers from 28 to 42 since 1891.

Let's again move forward for the last time.

References:

(1) Regulations for the Measuring and Photography of Criminal Prisoners SR & O 1896/762

Chapter Ten: 1911

The second Boer War had finished and the returning soldiers took up their old jobs. The treaty of Vereeniging confirmed British victory over the Boer republics after three years of war, and laid the foundations for the Union of South Africa. The cost and conduct of the war prompted concerns that Britain was no longer fit for its imperial role.

The Entente Cordiale agreement reconciled British and French imperial interests, particularly in Africa, but also marked the end of centuries of intermittent conflict and paved the way for future diplomatic and military cooperation. The two countries were united in their suspicion of Germany's ambitions.

The Edwardian era stood out as a time of peace and plenty. There were no severe depressions and prosperity was widespread. Britain's growth rate, manufacturing output, and GDP (but not per capita) fell behind its rivals the United States, and Germany. Nevertheless, the nation still led the world in trade, finance and shipping and had a strong base in both manufacturing and mining.

Politically, the Labour Party and the Women's Suffrage Movement made great strides. In 1908 Christabel Pankhurst was sentenced to a period in Holloway prison.

The law on drunkenness is tightened in 1902 and being drunk whilst responsible for a child was given a severe maximum sentence.

2.—(1) If any person is found drunk in any highway or other public place, whether a building or not, or on any licensed premises, while having the charge of a child apparently under the age of seven years, he may be apprehended, and shall, if the child is under that age, be liable on summary conviction to a fine not exceeding forty shillings, or to imprisonment, with or without hard labour, for any period not exceeding one month.

The sentencing of young offenders, 16-21 years old , was revised in the 1908 Crime Prevention Act (1) which aimed to send these offenders to a borstal institution for between 1 and 3 years. There was no guarantee that the offender would be allocated to the borstal nearest to their home. The act did provide financial resources to organisations who dealt with young people coming out of borstal.

The same act allowed the courts to apply an additional sentence when the defendant is proven to be a habitual offender. This could mean an extra 5-10 years of what was deemed preventative detention. If the prisoner was of

good behaviour after 3 years of the penal detention, some or all of the preventative detention may be commuted.

The next PM was **Arthur Balfour**, nephew of the Marquess of Salisbury. He served until 1905 but lost a landslide election early in 1906

He was replaced by the Liberal **Sir Henry Campbell-Bannerman.**

The Probation Act of 1907 allowed judges wide latitude to dismiss a charge tried summarily against a defendant even when the court thinks it is proved, or to conditionally discharge a defendant (whether the charge is tried summarily or on indictment). The power may be invoked when the court is of the opinion that having regard to the character, antecedents, age, health, or mental condition of the person charged, or to the trivial nature of the offence, or to the extenuating circumstances under which the offence was committed, it is inexpedient to inflict any punishment or that it is expedient to release the offender on probation. The application of the Act has occasionally caused controversy where victims or persons affected by the crime feel that the dismissal is inappropriate.

The next PM was another Liberal from Scotland, **Herbert Henry Asquith**, who was to remain in office until the outbreak of WW1.

The Old-Age Pensions Act 1908 is often regarded as one of the foundations of modern social welfare in the United Kingdom and forms part of the wider social welfare reforms of the Liberal Government.

Within Bedfordshire, politicians from North of the County reached important senior positions. Two Colworth men became Sheriffs of the County : William Clarence Watson in 1902 and Albert Edward Bowen in 1910. Six new magistrates were added to the Sharnbrook Division during the decade.

The Constabulary introduced a mounted police section in 1909. There are no records showing officers from Sharnbrook were used for this unit which was based at Headquarters.

Josselyn completed his 30 years service as the County's Chief Constable in 1910 and was replaced by Lt-Colonel Sir Frank Augustus Douglas Stevens.

John Nottingham was in office as

Inspector for the Sharnbrook Division for the whole decade. The inspector still had a 4 wheel cart; the first car was not to arrive until 1913. He would be followed by Inspector John Wilfred Bliss.

Sharnbrook provided constables for both the visit of King Edward VII to Wrest Park, Silsoe in 1909 and the docker's strike in Liverpool in 1911. They were not there long as the general railway strike meant that the men were recalled to protect signal boxes on the St Pancras line.

The MP for Bedford was a Liberal, Percy Barlow, who served until the first hung parliament in January 1910. He was followed by a Conservative, Walter Attenborough, who only served until December the same year.

The seventh of the national censuses was held on the 2nd April 1911 and Sharnbrook's registrar was Mr Williams and the enumerator was William Wootton. The census return on 189 schedules showed 755 residents, an increase of 10% from the 1901 survey. The gender distribution was 337 males and 418 females; the numbers under the age of 14 fell again to only 22%. Sharnbrook was now the second most populated village in North Beds. The highest population was still in Harrold. There had been a 10% decrease in the numbers of residents at Riseley. Sharnbrook was one of only 8 villages in the area which had seen an increase in population. The population of the North Bedfordshire villages had decreased by another 400 in the last ten years.

Using the 1903 trade directory the Sharnbrook tradesmen now included one postmaster, one baker, three Blacksmiths, two boot makers, four butchers, a saddler, a draper, a tailor, a dress maker, two plumbers, three millers, two carriers, two builders, seven farmers or bailiffs, a watchmaker, two coal merchants and a surgeon. There were also two publicans and a beer retailer, a builder, four gardeners, two laundry workers, one gamekeeper, a vicar, a station master, a brick maker and a school teacher.

In addition the census showed only 20 agricultural labourers. There were 37 residents recorded as skilled agricultural workers which is a decrease from 1901.

The numbers of residents employed in domestic service significantly increased to 115, up by 70%.

During the entirety of 1911 the Petty Sessions were held by one or more of 11magistrates

HBO Lord St John	RC Alston	AR Alston	R Orlebar
Whitworth	L Stileman-Gibbard	Dalton	Hipwell
C Pettit	Col S Jackson	MG Townley	RRB Orlebar

According to the Petty Session Minutes by far the most cases were again heard by Leonard Gibbard Stileman-Gibbard (31) with St John next on 24 cases. The fewest number of cases was heard by Alexander Rowland Alston.

The cases were distributed across the year

Jan - Mar	Apr- Jun	Jul- Sep	Oct - Dec	Total
30	9	6	20	65

The highest number of cases in any one session was 8, the lowest highest number seen to date in what is one very much the quietest year in the study period. Apart from May and August there were still regular session meetings on Fridays at fortnightly intervals.

The number of cases in 1911 classified by type

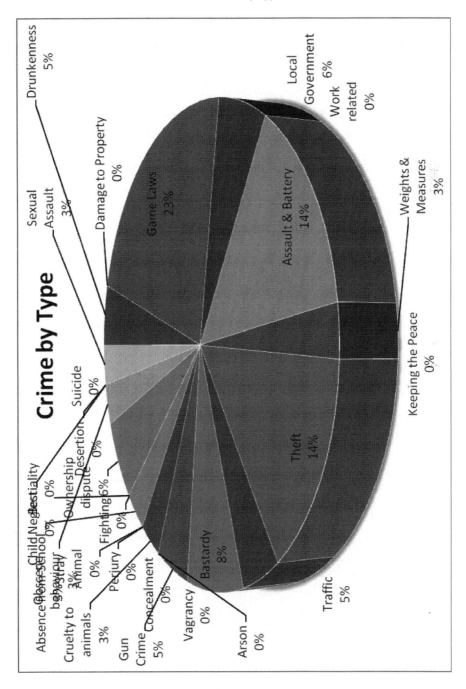

Crime by Type

Drunkenness 5%
Local Government 6%
Work related 0%
Sexual Assault 3%
Damage to Property 0%
Game Laws 23%
Assault & Battery 14%
Weights & Measures 3%
Suicide 0%
Keeping the Peace 0%
Theft 14%
Absence from School 0%
Closure 0%
Child Neglect 0%
Bestiality 0%
behaviour
Stray Animal 0%
Ownership dispute 0%
Desertion 0%
Fighting 6%
Cruelty to animals 3%
Gun 0%
Perjury 0%
Crime Concealment 5%
Vagrancy 0%
Bastardy 8%
Arson 0%
Traffic 5%

Assault cases nowstill only account for 14% and again but they are not the most common type of offence ; that position is now firmly taken by Game Law Offences at 23%. This time there are three associated cases of gun crime. Drunkenness is still very low .Theft has remained at a constant level. The number of Weights and Measures cases has remined at a very low level . There was a decrease in the new crime of Obscene Behaviour.

Not all cases resulted in guilty verdicts. The actual outcomes of the year's cases are shown

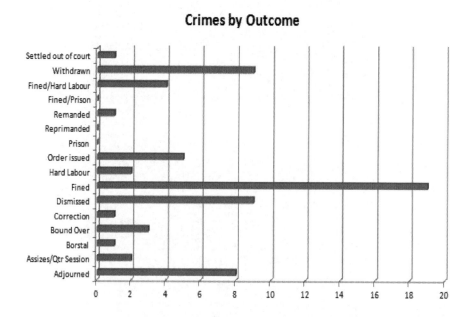

Crimes by Outcome

Imposition of a fine only had decreased to 19 cases (29%) whilst a further 4 (6%) cases were given a fine which if not paid would result in imprisonment with or without hard labour.

The details of the fines continue to show a breakdown into the two components:

- The value of any costs to witnesses / the constable

- A punitive fine to deter a repeat offence

The cases where a sentence of 'Fine or Prison' is recorded in the Court Minutes were generally still not formally resolved. Since there are no gaol records for this period we cannot confirm whether they failed to pay the fine. The number of cases 'withdrawn' or 'dismissed' was as high as 28%.

The court records show that only two cases were escalated to the Quarter Session/ Assizes. These included the case of James Orpin, a Northampton shoe finisher, who was accused of Night Poaching at Harrold and secondly, the case of Frank Day, accused of a sexual assault on a girl under 13 years old at Swineshead.

The gaol database does contain an earlier record for a James Orpin, also shown as a Shoe Finisher, who had a conviction for assault in 1890 and had served 1 month hard labour. This is further supported by the 1911 Census data where a James Orpen, born Harrold in 1869, is living in Castle Street, Northampton.

There are no earlier records for Frank Day in the gaol database however the 1911 census data shows that he lived at Straw's Yard, Irthlingborough with a wife and baby daughter.

The number of cases that were dismissed during this year fell to 14%. In only the second session of the year Charles Sykes was fortunate perhaps to have two cases withdrawn. He had been charged with stealing rugs value 16s 6d from the property of William Wise in Thurleigh. Also with stealing 4 rope wantys from William Green. If you look at the census data you see a completely different story for those records show he spent the census night in Bedford Gaol. The record confirms he was aged 23, a farmer from Thurleigh. The reason for the discrepancy is that at the same petty session he was convicted of stealing 8 live turkeys, value £6, from William Payne in Bletsoe and received a sentence of 4 months hard labour. A co-defendant, George Mathers, was also found guilty and was sentenced to 2 months hard labour so he was out of gaol before the census. One other co-defendant,

John Osborn, was bound over and the case against a fourth defendant, Frank Foskett, was dismissed.

In March, James Smith faced two charges of Poaching at Felmersham. Both cases were prosecuted by the gamekeeper, Thomas Betts. James was given two identical sentences of a fine of £1 & 4s3d costs or 14 days hard labour. His co defendant, Herbert Willsher, faced charges of Poaching and Assault but failed to appear in court. A warrant was issued and the case adjourned but there is no record of him appearing in this calendar year.

The new Weights and Measures Inspector, Arthur Poole, prosecuted William Smart, for using a false weighing instrument in Sharnbrook. A second charge of using an unstamped weighing machine followed. He was fined 10s for each offence.

In April, Frank Meekham was convicted of house breaking at Pavenham and stealing £1 16s and goods valued at 4s. He was sentenced to 8 months within the Brick Road. Another report showed that he was sentenced to 8 strokes with the birch and then handed over to Reformatory authorities. The census data showed Frank Meecham, aged 14, at Carlton Reformatory. He was recorded as being a farm hand, born in Lambeth, London.

William Bridgeford and George Dilley were co-defendants on a charge of poaching at Yielden in August. The magistrates Gibbard and Whitworth dismissed the cases because the prosecution summons had referred to the wrong Act. A month later the two men were in court again facing a charge of carrying a gun without a licence and the date of the offence was given as the same as the prior case. This time they were both fined £5 and 8s 6d costs.

There was complex set of cases in October; William Charles Knight faced one charge of assault from Frederick Pettit and one charge of shooting with intent to commit grievous bodily harm from Arthur Pettit. To counter this Knight was also prosecuting both of the Pettits for assault. The magistrates obviously did a lot of reconciliation behind the scenes because all assault charges were eventually withdrawn and Knight was bound over on a surety of £10 for good behaviour for 12 months.

An inmate of Carlton Reformatory was again the defendant in two cases in November. Tom Mellor was charged both with escaping custody and breaking into a house and stealing clothing in Harrold. The census records for the Reformatory show a Tom Millor, aged 16, a carpenter from Boston, Lincs. The theft charge was withdrawn but he was sentenced to 3 years at Borstal for the other case.

Also in November, William Barnes faced two charges; one of drunkenness in a licensed premises and one of using obscene language in the highway. The publican at The Jackal, Thurleigh, Peter Horn, was also charged with permitting drunkenness in his premises. All three defendants received fines of between 10s and £2.

Did the cases held in Sharnbrook Petty Session get into the local press? The answer is again definitely YES but the coverage is less than the previous years since only 62% of cases were reported. Again many of the reports just summarised the case by describing the defendant, the nature of the offence and the outcome.

The case against Sykes et al for stealing turkeys was described in detail and showed that Foskett was away at work when the other defendants left the turkeys in the outhouse at his Clapham home. The other three defendants pleaded guilty but the magistrates recognised the Osborn was only doing what his master had required of him hence he received no imprisonment.

The report on the case against James Orpin described how two gamekeepers were waiting in fields at Gusset's Corner and heard a gunshot at 1:45am; they then saw 4 men walk along the hedgerow and the second man carried a double-barrelled gun. The gamekeepers gave chase and Orpin was caught by a blow to his head as he tried to climb a fence. The game keepers collected cartridges and two pheasants from the scene and took Orpin to the doctors at Harrold and then to the Police Inspector at Sharnbrook. A later report described Orpin as the most notorious poacher in the district and that he had 69 previous convictions although none of them involved use of a gun as a weapon of offence. He is reported as promising the magistrate he would not go poaching any more so the magistrate took a lenient view and he was sentenced to 2 months hard labour.

Another complex report covered the series of poaching cases against James Smith. He pleaded guilty on a charge of poaching and admitted an assault on the gamekeeper but asked for leniency because he had only just got out of prison and the Discharged Prisoners Aid Society were trying to arrange him to go to sea to make a man of him. The magistrates decided to hear the second series of repeat charges against him before reaching a decision. His defence was much the same. The magistrates decided that because he had so many previous convictions they had to give him a custodial sentence but believing him to be in earnest they were lenient in giving him only half the normal sentence. He could not pay the fines hence received 14 days for each case.

The report of the Weights and Measure case against William Smart described how he was a Butcher from Rushden who was seen using the offending scales in Souldrop and Colworth. The Inspector decribed how the scales were in error by one ounce up to the weight of 7lb. The defendant claimed that the scales had belonged to his predecessor. The Inspector explained that the requirements for testing scales were published and, in addition to the fine, the court ordered that the scales be forfeited.

The report on the cases against Bridgeford and Dilley described how the two men managed to separate the barrel and the stock of the gun so that each of them had a part of the weapon when apprehended by Police Sergeant Dennis and PC Stevens at Yielden. Since there was no evidence that the weapon had been used for poaching the cases were dismissed but with the caveat that they were still likely to be charged under a different act.

Who had brought the case against the defendants?

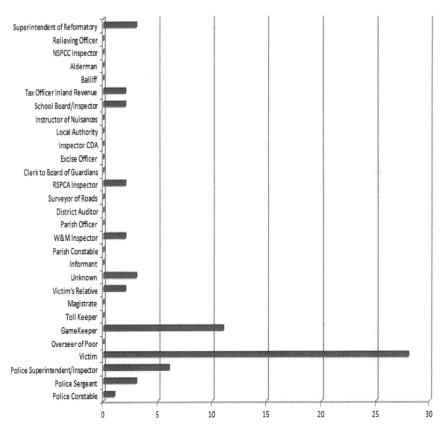

The number of cases prosecuted by the Victim was still the highest at 28 (43%) which is as high a proportion seen throughout the study period. The proportion of case brought by a police officer has again decreased to 15%. The role of gamekeeper now accounts for 11 cases (17%). There are again no prosecutions by a Parish Constable. We do see another increase in the number of different roles named as the plaintiff; many of these new roles are inspectors with specific responsibilities for areas of community health/welfare /taxation and for the first time we see prosecutions by the Superintendent of the Carlton Reformatory.

The annual inspections by the HMIC continued to be a routine event however the report for 1911 is not available.

That's all the study years complete. We will use the next chapter to analyse for any trends across the years before doing a detailed study of poaching and theft.

References:

(1) Prevention of Crime Act 1908 c59

Chapter Eleven: Trends across the Years 1841-1911

In the preceding chapters we have studied in some detail the nature of the crimes committed in the second year of the decade which happened to be the same year as the national census. We occasionally commented on whether a particular level of crime was an increase or decrease over the previous decade. Can we see any more patterns/trends in the local court records?

Cases of Crime in Petty Session Court

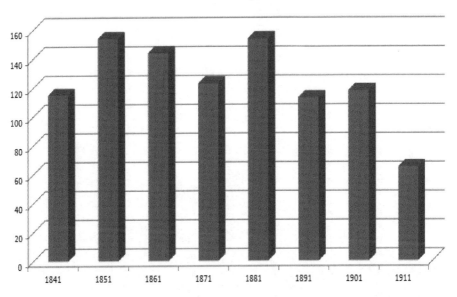

The total number of cases seen in The Bletsoe/Sharnbrook court shows two peaks in 1851 and 1881.

Distribution of cases across the year

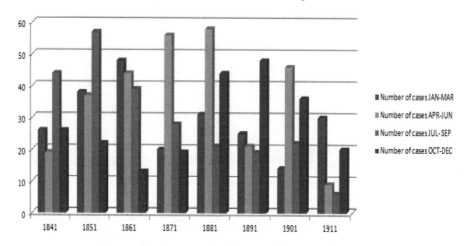

Throughout the study period the greatest number of cases was heard in the April-June period. This is certainly true in the peak of 1881whereas in 1851 there were more cases between July and September. Overall, the fewest cases were heard in October- December but even then this was the lowest quarter in only 3 of the 8 study years.

Maximum number of cases per session

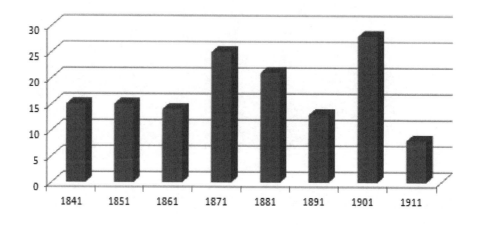

The maximum number of cases in any one session was seen 1901 and the second was in 1871. Neither corresponded with the years where there were the highest case numbers.

The total case number for the study period was 986 and these were classified into 28 different types of crime.

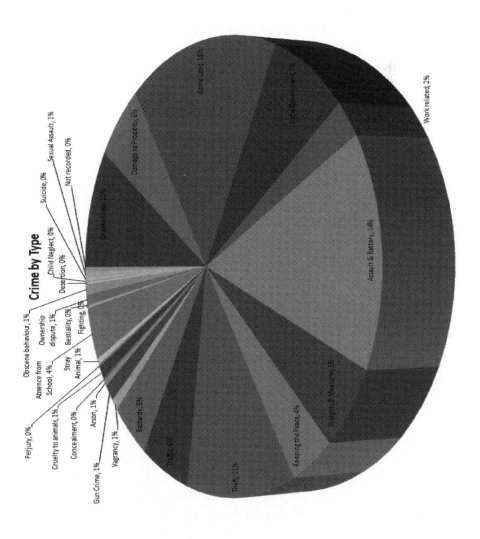

The highest number of cases is in the category of Game Laws, which accounted for 16% of all cases. The next most common were Assault at 14%, Theft at 11% and Drunkenness at 10%. It is of course likely that many of the assault cases involved a scenario where the defendant was also drunk.

The bulk of the 4% of cases relating to absence from School contributes significantly to the peak of the activity in 1881. This period demonstrates the rigour of the inspection system set up within the 1880 Education Act and shows how a local initiative can influence statistics when the population of data is relatively small.

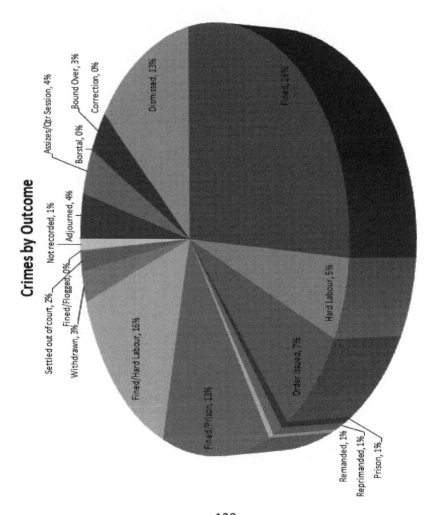

Not all these cases resulted in a guilty verdict. Only 4% of cases were inconclusive i.e. adjourned. 13% of cases were dismissed and a further 3% were withdrawn.

The most usual outcome for the 84% of cases that were proven was simply a fine. The fact that a sentence of transportation was not seen in the earlier years is just a reflection of the low level of crime seen in North Bedfordshire in the Victorian era. Even more of the cases were given a sentence that required the defendant to go to prison if the fine was not paid. In more case than not, the prison option included hard labour. The point was to make the work hard and deliberately degrading: to break the prisoner's will and self-respect. There was a policy of 'Hard bed, hard board, hard labour'. In the last part of the 19th century, after the 1865 Prisons Act and under Assistant Director of Prisons Sir Edmund du Cane, prisons were made even tougher. Hard plank beds replaced hammocks, food was deliberately boring and inmates had to work hard on the monotonous tasks such as the crank. This was a large handle in each cell, with a counter. The prisoner had to do so many thousand turns a day. Warders could tighten up the crank, making it harder to turn.

The escalation of defendants to appear before the Quarter Session of the Assizes was recorded in only 4% of cases but we have seen that not all these cases subsequently appear on the Quarter Session prisoner lists or in the list of indictments. More than a half of all escalated cases were in 1851.

The relationship between the plaintiff and the defendant was studied using a combination of court records, census data and newspaper report and a rudimentary classification scheme was created.

Nature of the Plaintiff

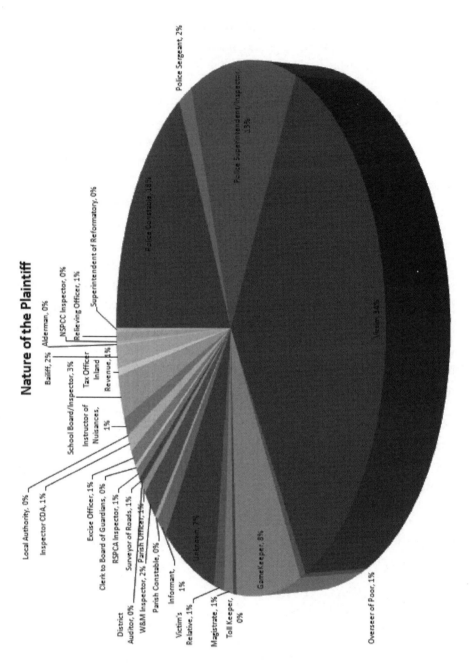

The data shows that the victim was the plaintiff in 34% of all cases. There was no overall trend since the proportion of cases prosecuted by the victim was high in 1851, 1861 and 1891 but low in 3 other years.

Cases where Victim was the plaintiff

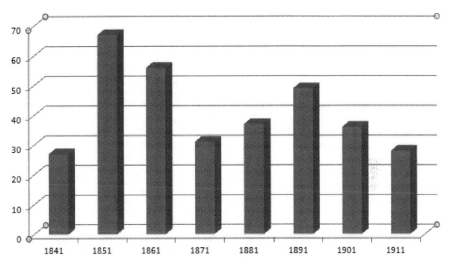

Since the most cases were classified as Game Law offences it is interesting to see how many cases were prosecuted by the gamekeepers. Prior to 1861 it appears that Game Law cases were prosecuted by the land owners but from 1861 onwards the gamekeepers acted as the land owner's representative. We have seen many cases where the gamekeeper was not only the main witness but the person who caught and held the accused until the police

Cases where Game Keeper was the plaintiff

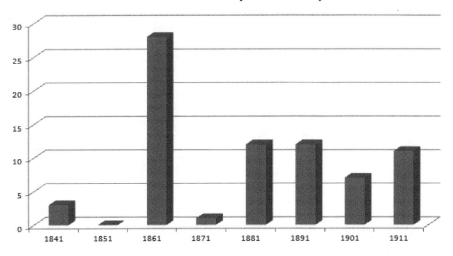

arrived.

Of the total of 986 cases a study of the gaol database shows that about 10% of cases resulted in the defendant spending a period in Bedford Gaol. Some of these were direct convictions of imprisonment or hard labour, particularly for theft, whilst many were the result of the defendant not being able to pay the imposed fine. It was also possible that a few records just reflected the stay in prison awaiting appearance at the Quarter Session or Assizes at which their case may have been dismissed or they would return to gaol to serve their sentence.

The gaol database and the new Quarter Session index are formidable sources of crime numbers. For the period 1830 -1899 the gaol database contains just over 40,000 records. The distribution across the decades shows the greatest number of gaol residents in 1850-59.

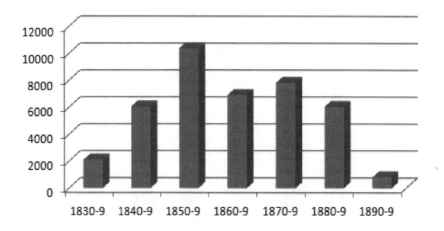

Number of Records in Bedford Gaol database

Gaol records during Study Years

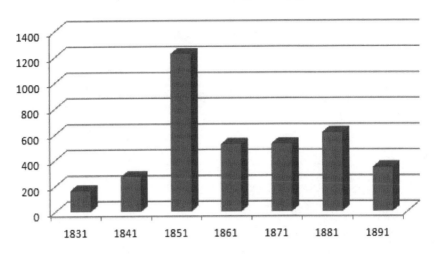

A similar pattern is seen if you analyse just the gaol residents in the census years. There were 1222 people in gaol during the peak of 1851.

27% of all gaol records contained the word 'steal' in the description of the offence and again the peak was seen in the 1850-59 period. The sentencing of repeat offenders to harsher i.e. longer gaol sentences is evident in the

database records. The case of **Henry Mackness** is a good example. Henry was born in Wymington and served his first sentence in 1864 when he was convicted of house breaking and stealing 2 pairs of trousers. He was sentenced to two periods of 6 month hard labour to run concurrently.

He was back in court again in 1866 as **Henry Machness** and was convicted of stealing 15 fowl from the property of John Ivell in Bedford. He was sentenced to 7 year penal servitude and after a time in Bedford was removed to Pentonville. Eight years later he again is accused of two accounts of stealing fowl and of night poaching. This time he is acquitted but he obviously spent time in the gaol since he was discharged the day after the trial.

The QSR index for the same period contains 32,277 records and 38% of them contain the word 'steal' in the description of the offence.

Number of records in QSR

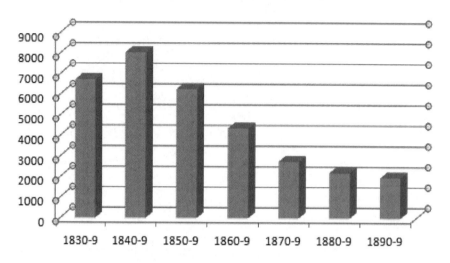

The highest number of QS cases occurred in the 1840-49 decade but the highest number of Theft cases was in the 1850-59 decade.

The overall number of gaol records and QS cases relating to Game Laws will be covered in the next chapter.

It will come as no surprise that 29% of all Sharnbrook Division cases were heard by magistrates named St John or Orlebar. Their families' contribution to the provision of law and order in North Bedfordshire has been immense.

The coverage of petty session cases in the local newspaper went through a step change in the 1850s.

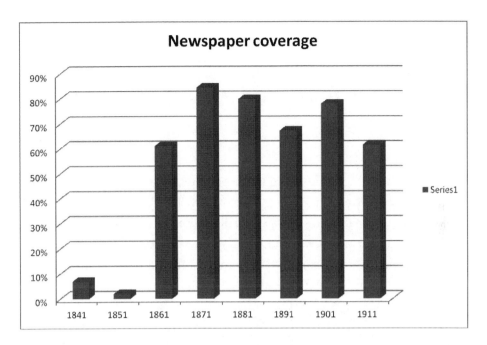

Newspaper coverage

The highest level of reporting was seen in 1871 but it remained at a high level throughout the second half of the study period.

Chapter Twelve: Poaching

Poaching is commonly portrayed as the archetypal nineteenth-century 'rural' crime, particularly associated with agricultural districts of southern and eastern England. Poaching was a crime often linked to poverty, but its seasonal timing usually owed more to practical considerations concerning both the suitability of the natural environment for hunting and the availability, maturity and marketability of the quarry. Around Bedfordshire rabbits or conies were often the target and unlike some species, rabbits and hares were ever present, albeit in varying numbers, throughout the year. However, like game birds, rabbits appeared in greater numbers after harvest and, as with partridges, it was also necessary for the fields to be clear before certain forms of poaching such as coursing or netting could be effective. Those poachers and commercial warreners, who take rabbits from beneath ground, usually did so between November and February during the brief winter pause in the rabbit's reproductive activity. Rabbits and hares also have the advantage that they can be sold without a licence.

Images of a poacher and gamekeepers from the Victorian era

Historians have always considered it particularly significant that the majority of offences were committed between October and March, a period when outdoor labour was most prone to interruption, demand for farm labour was slackest and therefore poverty most acute.

There were a series of Game Law Acts in our study period.

The Night Poaching Act 1828 is an Act of the Parliament of the United Kingdom (citation 9 Geo. IV c. 69) still in effect in the 21st century. It forbids night poaching, especially taking or destroying game on lands, etc., by night, or entering lands at night to take or destroy game.

For the purposes of this Act the word "game" was deemed to include hares, pheasants, partridges, grouse, heath or moor game, black game, and bustards. The severity of the sentences listed in the Act clearly shows the government's determination to combat the growth in this particular crime. A first offender is sentenced to 3 months hard labour and on release has to pay surety of £10 against re-offending in the following 12 months. If the surety is not paid the offender has to serve a further 6 months. For a second offence all the terms are doubled to 6 months hard labour plus surety of £20 against re-offending in two years. If the surety is not paid the offender has to serve a further 12 months. For a third offence the sentence is 7 years transportation or 2 years hard labour. The gaol record for **George Denton** showed he

Gaol Record Detail For: George Denton

Record ID:	46441
Commital Year:	1891
Reference Doc:	BLARS PRIS2/2/5
ID in Reference Doc:	7919
Age:	20
Gender:	Male
Height:	5 feet 7 inches
Hair Colour:	Light Brown
Occupation:	Shoe finisher
Education:	Imperfect
Form of Religion:	Church of England
Birth Town:	Rushden
Offence:	Night poaching
When Committed:	12/06/1891
Type of Gaol:	Bedford Gaol
Sentence:	2 calendar months hard labour and sureties or 6 calendar months further
How Disposed:	Found sureties
Discharge Date:	11/08/1891

managed to pay the surety and hence avoid the longer period of hard labour.

The less specific Game Law of 1831 served as a major update of many historical laws. In fact the preamble to the act listed approximately 30 previous statutes dating back to the reign of Richard II and including some as recent as from the last years of the long reign of George III. This Act reaffirmed the land owners right to take the game and their authority to permit others to take the game; it also set defined seasons for different game birds. It enabled the landowner to appoint gamekeepers and set penalties for the unauthorised taking of game or for the possession of such game.

An article in the Huntingdon, Bedford and Peterborugh Gazette in 1832 described how there had been a major incident involving up to 30 poachers and a similar number of gamekeepers at Pytchley. The conflict resulted in a large loss of blood on both sides. The poachers who were detained had previous convictions and were considered as commercial criminals rather than opportunists.

The Poaching Prevention Act 1862 allowed police officers to stop and search anyone on the road for evidence of poaching. (In theory, this was allowed only if the suspect was coming from a game preservation area.) Previously the stop and search authority had come from the 1824 Vagrancy Act.

What trends can we see in the data from our study period? Does it reflect the above assumptions and predictions?

Taking our overall figures from the study period we saw that 162 cases out of the total of 986 were in the category of Game Law offences equating to 16% of cases. In this category we have grouped all offences under any of the above statutes.

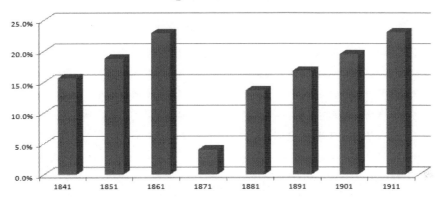

Percentage of Game Law offences

The highest number of cases (33) was seen in 1861 and the highest percentage of cases (23%) was seen in both 1861 and 1911. The lowest number (5) and the lowest percentage (4%) occurred in 1871.

We have already seen how the role of gamekeeper was important as a plaintiff in this type of offence. This was not just for the more serious Night Poaching cases but included other cases dealt by the summary court. There is evidence that gamekeepers acted collaboratively manner to protect their different game preserves. The records do also include statements from persons described as 'watchers' who had the same authority as the gamekeeper when apprehending a poacher.

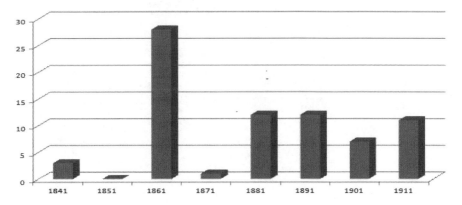

Cases where Game Keeper was the plaintiff

The peak of prosecution by a Game keeper was in 1861when they were the plaintiff in 28 of the 33 Game Law cases.

A book published in 1851 can be considered the gamekeeper's rule book (1). The early chapters describe the gamekeeper's skill in preserving different species. It then gives observation on poaching and the means of preventing it. The book has a strong condemnation of the poachers way of life and provides a vivid description of the poacher as a villain who "is at variance with any other class of human species". The poacher is said to "generally exhibit external marks of characteristics of his profession; the suspicious leer of this hollow and sunken eyes, his pallid cheek, his wide, copious and well-pocketed jacket". The act of poaching is described as "demoralising, debasing and disgusting and generally relates in ill-health to the poacher as well as the threat of imprisonment or transportation".

What were the outcomes of these 162 cases?

Only 12% of cases were withdrawn or dismissed. 39% of cases were either directly given a sentence with hard labour or were given a fine which if they could not pay would result in hard labour. This may even be an underestimate because sometimes the court record states the length of the sentence but not the additional hardship. A comparison with gaol records

Game Law cases by Outcome

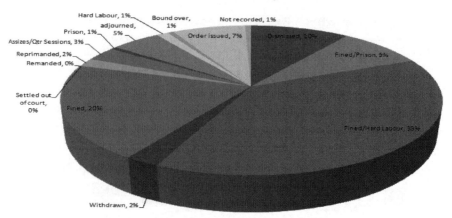

and newspaper reports showed the imprisonment did often include the additional conditions of hardship. Therefore some of the 9% of cases where the non-payment of fine would lead to imprisonment may well have included hard labour. Over the whole study period for all types of offence the outcome of Hard Labour or Fine / Hard Labour was decided in 21% of cases.

Back to Game Laws: the sentence of just a fine was seen in 20% of cases but the less harsh outcomes e.g. bound over, are hardly ever used.

Using a pivot table it is possible to see the range of sentences given to any chosen type of crime. We have used this to study the variation in sentencing for Game Law Offences.

⊕ Game Laws	18
Dismissed on paying 4s and 3s costs	1
Dismissed with reprimand	1
Fined £2 or 2 months prison	1
Fined £2 plus 12s6d fees plus 5s costs or 2 months Hard Labour	1
Fined £2 plus costs	1
Fined £3 plus 12s6d fees plus 5s costs or 2 months Hard Labour	1
Fined £5 or 3 months prison	1
Fined £5 plus £ 6s costs or 3months hard labour	1
Fined £5 plus £1 10s costs , eventually committed to prison for 3 months	1
Fined £5 plus 3s 6d constble fe plus £1 6s cost or 3 months hard labour	1
Fined 10s	3
Fined 1s plus 17s 6d costs or 1 month Hard Labour	1
Fined 1s plus 1s service costs plus 13s costs or 14 days hard labour	1
Fined 9s plus 1s to constable plus 10s costs	1
Fined undisclosed amount plus costs	1
Reprimanded plus 7s 6d costs	1

For Game Law offences in 1841 there are many outcomes ranging from dismissal through to a fine of £5 where failure to pay would result in 3 months hard labour.

By 1851 we have 3 dismissals but the number of outcomes involving hard labour has increased and the maximum is now 10 months hard labour

Adjourned	2
case not heard since Pettit on another charge	1
Committed to prison	1
Dismissed	3
Fined £1 10s plus 15s costs or 6 weeks hard labour	1
Fined £1 10s 6d plus 13s 6d or 6 weeks hard labour	2
Fined £1 8s 6d plus 15s 6d costs	1
Fined £1 plus 15s 6d costs or 3 weeks hard labour	1
Fined £2 plus £1 police costs or 2 months hard labour	1
Fined £5 plus 19s 6d costs or 2 months prison	1
Fined £5 plus 19s 6d costs or 3 months hard labour	2
Fined 10s 6d	1
Fined 10s 6d plus 9s 6d costs or 3 weeks hard labour	1
Fined 10s plus 15s6d costs or 14 days hard labour	1
Fined 4s 6d plus 15s costs or 3 weeks hard labour	1
Fined 5s 6d	1
Fined 6s plus 2s damage plus 4s costs	1
Fined 8s 6d plus 16s6d costs or 3 weeks hard labour	1
Fined 9s 6d plus 15s 6d costs or 3 weeks hard labour	1
Reprimanded plus 10s 6d costs	1
Sent to Assizes, 1 month Hard Labour	1
Sent to Assizes, 10 months hard labour	1
Sent to Assizes. Bail of £10 plus 1X surety of £10; acquitted	2

By now we have already come across Jesse Green. His list of convictions which are predominantly for poaching shows him to be a habitual criminal.

Personal details

Height: 5 ft 6 ½ inches

Hair colour: Brown

Eye colour: Hazel

Visage: Oval

Complexion: Fresh

Identifying marks: Cut mark under left eye, right arm crippled, freckled face.

Trade or occupation: Rat Catcher

Education: Imp

Marriage status: Married

Number of children: Unknown

Religion: Church of England

Residence details

Birth town: Thurleigh

Birth country: England

Residence town: Thurleigh

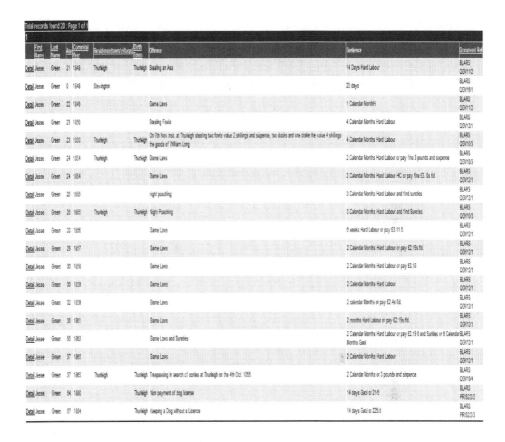

	First Name	Last Name	Age	Committal Year	Residence/town/village	Birth Town	Offence	Sentence	Document Ref
Detail	Jesse	Green	21	1849	Thurleigh	Thurleigh	Stealing an Ass	14 Days Hard Labour	BLARS QGV11/2
Detail	Jesse	Green	0	1849	Stevington			21 days	BLARS QGV15/1
Detail	Jesse	Green	22	1849			Game Laws	1 Calendar MonthH	BLARS QGV11/2
Detail	Jesse	Green	23	1850			Stealing Fowls	4 Calendar Months Hard Labour	BLARS QGV12/1
Detail	Jesse	Green	23	1850	Thurleigh	Thurleigh	On 7th Nov inst. at Thurleigh stealing two fowls value 2 shillings and sixpence, two ducks and one drake the value 4 shillings the goods of William Long	4 Calendar Months Hard Labour	BLARS QGV10/3
Detail	Jesse	Green	24	1854	Thurleigh	Thurleigh	Game Laws	2 Calendar Months Hard Labour or pay fine 3 pounds and sixpence	BLARS QGV10/3
Detail	Jesse	Green	24	1854			Game Laws	2 Calendar Months Hard Labour HC or pay fine £3. 0s 6d	BLARS QGV12/1
Detail	Jesse	Green	25	1855			night poaching	3 Calendar Months Hard Labour and find sureties	BLARS QGV12/1
Detail	Jesse	Green	25	1855	Thurleigh	Thurleigh	Night Poaching	3 Calendar Months Hard Labour and find Sureties	BLARS QGV10/3
Detail	Jesse	Green	26	1856			Game Laws	6 weeks Hard Labour or pay £3.11.6	BLARS QGV12/1
Detail	Jesse	Green	29	1857			Game Laws	2 Calendar Months Hard Labour or pay £2.19s.6d.	BLARS QGV12/1
Detail	Jesse	Green	30	1858			Game Laws	2 Calendar Months Hard Labour or pay £3.18	BLARS QGV12/1
Detail	Jesse	Green	30	1859			Game Laws	2 Calendar Months Hard Labour	BLARS QGV12/1
Detail	Jesse	Green	32	1859			Game Laws	2 calendar Months or pay £2.4s 6d.	BLARS QGV12/1
Detail	Jesse	Green	35	1861			Game Laws	2 months Hard Labour or pay £2.19s.6d.	BLARS QGV12/1
Detail	Jesse	Green	55	1863			Game Laws and Sureties	2 Calendar Months Hard Labour or pay £2.19.6 and Sureties or 6 Calendar Months Gaol	BLARS QGV12/1
Detail	Jesse	Green	37	1865			Game Laws	2 Calendar Months Hard Labour	BLARS QGV12/1
Detail	Jesse	Green	37	1865	Thurleigh	Thurleigh	Trespassing in search of conies at Thurleigh on the 4th Oct. 1865	2 Calendar Months or 3 pounds and sixpence	BLARS QGV19/4
Detail	Jesse	Green	54	1880		Thurleigh	Non payment of dog license	14 days Gaol or 21/6	BLARS PRIS2/2
Detail	Jesse	Green	57	1884		Thurleigh	Keeping a Dog without a Licence	14 days Gaol or 22/6d	BLARS PRIS2/3

As such he was one of the few prisoners who were photographed at Bedford Gaol. You can see that he was found guilty of Game Law offences on 11 separate occasions between 1849 and 1865. He served many sentences of 2-3 months hard labour.

Interestingly Jesse's two convictions for theft in 1850 received the more severe sentence of 4 month hard labour.

In the interim years a labourer living in Sharnbrook was sentenced to 3 months hard labour. James White, aged 54, was summarily convicted and served 3 months hard labour.

Gaol Record Detail For: James White

Record ID:	12640
Commital Year:	1855
Reference Doc:	BLARS QGV10/3
ID in Reference Doc:	3765
Age:	54
Gender:	Male
Height:	5 feet 2 inches
Hair Colour:	Grey
Eye Colour:	Grey
Complexion:	Fresh
Visage:	Oval
Occupation:	Labourer
Education:	Read and Write
Marital Status:	Married
Birth Town:	Pulloxhill
Birth County:	Bedfordshire
Residence(town/village):	Sharnbrook
Residence(county):	Bedfordshire
Offence:	Game Laws
Committed By:	Charles Moore Esquire and Rev.G.G.Harter
When Committed:	22/11/1855
Trial Type:	Summarily Convicted
Type of Gaol:	Bedford County Gaol
Sentence:	3 Calendar Months Hard Labour or pay6 pounds 8 shillings
Discharge Date:	21/02/1856

In 1860 we see that a poacher from Hertfordshire was tempted to commit a felony in the Luton area. George Bennett, alias Henry Simpson, was a 28 year old poacher with a long of previous convictions.

Each time he had been jailed for two or three months, but in September 1860 he lashed out at the constable arresting him and was given two years for assault.

A butcher by trade, he was 5ft 10in with dark hair and grey eyes. A Roman Catholic who could barely read, he had an anchor, bird and heart tattoo on his left arm, and had lost the little finger on his left hand.

His convictions on poaching started in 1846 at age 12.

No. of Previous Convictions:	19
Previous Conviction Details:	St. Albans, 1845 Mch 15, Wilful Damage, 1 Month, 1845 Apr 15, Poaching, Discharged, Watford, 1846 Apr 17, Stealing a trap, Not guilty, 1847 May 25, Poaching, Discharged, 1847 Oct 5, Poaching, Discharged, 1848, Jan 24, Poaching, 2 months, 1848 May 9, Poaching, Discharged, 1848 Oct 23 Poaching, 2 months, 1848 Dec 23, Poaching, 2 months, 1849 Feb 24, Stealing fowl, Discharged, 1849 July 31, pound breach, fined 7 shillings and costs, 1849 Sep 18, Riot in a beerhouse, Sureties for 6 months, Hemel Hempstead, 1849 Nov 14, Poaching, £2 and costs, Watford, 1849 Nov 26, Poaching, 3 months, Watford, 1850 Apr 27, Poaching, 2 months, Watford, 1850 Oct 16, Poaching, 2 months, Watford, 1851 Feb 10, Poaching, 2 months, Herts summer assizes, Night Poaching, 9 calender months, Watford, 1853 May 17, Common Assault, 1 month, 1853 Nov 3, Poaching, fined 4£ and costs, St. Albans, 1854 Jan 3, Assaulting Police, 2 years, Hertford, 1853 summer assizes, Highway Robbery, 3 calender months, 1856 Mch 7, Poaching, 2 calender months, Herts, 1856 May 13, Night Poaching 4 years. PS
How Disposed:	Discharged
Discharge Date:	15/10/1862
Photograph Ref:	qgv10-4-21.JPG

In 1861 the outcomes included 11 instances where the defendant failed to appear and orders were issued for the accused to be arrested. This contributes a definite positive bias to the count of how many actual instances of poaching there were in this year. A fine or a period of hard labour between 1 and 3 months is still the norm.

Game Laws	33
adjourned	2
Dismisssed	1
Fined £1 plus 10s 6d to police and witness plus £15s 6d costs or 3 weeks hard labour	1
Fined £1 plus 16s 6d costs or 1 month in prison	1
Fined £2 plus £10s 6d costs or 2 months hard labour	3
Fined £2 plus £10s 6d costs or 6 weeks hard labour	3
Fined £2 plus £11s 6d costs or 2 months hard labour	3
Fined £2 plus £15s costs or 2 monthshard labour	1
Fined £2 plus 16s 6d costs or 1 month prison	1
Fined £5 plus 16s 6d costs or 3 months in prison	1
Fined 5s plus 16s6d costs or 1 month hard labour	2
Fined 5s plus 19s6d costs or 14 days hard labour	1
Fined costs	1
Summons issued	9
Unknown	1
warrant issued	2

In 1871 there are very few game Law cases and the maximum sentence is a £5 fine or 2 weeks hard labour.

Game Laws
Dismissed
Fined £5 0s 8d
Fined 5s plus 16s costs or 14 days hard labour
Fined 5s plus 9s costs or 14 days hard labour

In 1881 the maximum sentence maximum sentence is reduced to £3 fine and 1 month hard labour.

Game Laws	21
Dismissed	2
Fined £15s plus 13s/6d costs or unspeciified period of hard labour	1
Fined £1 plus 14s/6d costs or 1 month hard labour	2
Fined £1 plus 14s/6d costs or 1 month in prison	1
Fined £1 plus 14s/6d costs or 1 month in prison to follow previous conviction	3
Fined £1 plus 9s/6d costs or unspeciified period of hard labour	1
Fined £2 plus 12s/6d costs or 1 month hard labour	1
Fined £2 plus 13s/6d costs or unspeciified period of hard labour	1
Fined £2 plus 14s/6d costs or 1 month hard labour	1
Fined £2 plus 9s/6d costs or 1 month hard labour	2
Fined 10s plus 7s/6d costs or 14 days hard labour	3
Fined 20s plus 8s/6d costs or 1 month hard labour	2
Fined 31 plus 9s/6d costs or 1 month hard labour	1

In 1891 the maximum sentence has increased to £5 and 2 months hard labour. There were more cases where the outcome was a fine only.

⊞ Game Laws	19
2 months Hard Labour	1
Case dismissed	3
Committed for 2 months, bound over £10 plus £2 plus £5 for 12 months	1
Fined £1 and 11s costs or 1 month imprisonment	1
Fined £1 and 11s costs or 1 month imprisonment plus gun to be destroyed	1
Fined £3 plus costs 7s/10d, allowed 14days to pay	1
Fined £5 plus 10s/6d costs or 2 months Hard Labour	2
Fined £5 plus 12s/6d costs or 2 months Hard Labour	1
Fined 10s plus 12s costs	1
Fined 10s plus 12s6d	1
Fined 10s plus 7s/10d costs	1
Fined 10s plus 7s/10d costs , allowed 14 days to pay	3
Fined 2s plus 9s/6d costs or 7 days Hard Labour	1
Fined 2s/6d plus 7s/6d costs	1

In 1901 the maximum sentence is 2 months hard labour.

⊞ Game Laws	22
Case withdrawn on payment of costs 4s	1
Committed to HM Prison for 2 months Hard labour	1
Defendant did not appear, warrant issued	1
Dismissed	1
Fined £1 incl costs	2
Fined £1 plus 7s/6d costs	1
Fined £2 plus 12s6d costs or 1 month Hard Labour	2
Fined £2 plus 19s/9d costs or 1 month Hard Labour	1
Fined £2 plus 7s6d costs	2
Fined 10s and 7s/6d costs or 14 days in prison	1
Fined 10s incl costs	1
Fined 10s plus 11s costs	1
Fined 31 plus 12s costs or 14days Hard Labour to run concurrently with 2 other terms of imprisonment	1
Fined 5s and 7s/6d costs	1
Fined 5s plus 8s/6d costs	1
Fined 7s6d plus 7s6d costs	1
Withdrawn	2
Withdrawn on payment of costs	1

The 1911 there were more dismissals and the maximum sentence was a fine of £2 and 1 month hard labour.

Game Laws	15
Adjourned for 6 weeks	1
Committed to trial at insuing Bedford Assizes	1
Defendant not yet apprehended	1
Dismissed	1
Dismissed on payment of 5s costs plus defendants father undertaking to destroy the dog	1
Dismissed, summons under wrong Act	2
Fined £1 & 4s/3d costs or 14 days hard labour	2
Fined £1 incl costs	3
Fined £2 and 8s/6d costs or 1 month hard labour	2
No appearance, warrant issued, adjourned	1

Using only the years in this study period we can see that the harshest sentences were issued in the earlier years especially 1851.

Do we see the same trends if we use the gaol database? We can of course only study the period up to 1898 but we can include the decade immediately before our own study period.

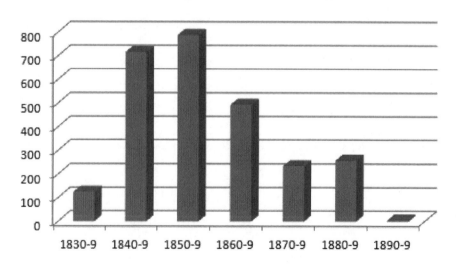

Game Law Imprisonments by decade

Here the peak period for sentences for offences classified specifically as Game Laws is the 1850 decade when there were 788 cases. The total number of records was 2619. In addition the database includes two other classifications which are relevant. One classification is called Night Poaching and this has another 248 records.

This peak period differs markedly from national statistics where data collected after 1858 show that poaching prosecutions in England continued to rise throughout the 1860s from around 9,000 in 1860 to just over 11,700 ten years later. After dipping sharply in the early 1870s to just over 8,600, they then resumed their upward trend, peaking in 1877 at just under 12,400 cases. After that, despite temporary reversals, the data shows a steady national decline, with cases virtually halving over the next twenty-five years.(2)

The dramatic peak in day prosecutions that occurred in the late 1870s can be explained entirely by reference to a relatively small number of counties in the North and Midlands. Between 1872 and 1876 prosecutions for day poaching rose by 167 per cent in Northumberland, 125 per cent in Durham, 114 per cent in Lancashire, ninety-nine per cent in the West Riding of Yorkshire, eighty-three per cent in Northamptonshire, eighty two per cent in Warwickshire, eighty per cent in Derby, seventy-two per cent in Staffordshire, sixty-six per cent in Cheshire, sixty-four per cent in Nottinghamshire and fifty-nine per cent in Leicestershire. Industrialising counties were also responsible for the equally dramatic fall in prosecutions from the late 1870s By contrast, prosecutions in the agricultural South and East failed to reflect national trends. During the late 1870s they were consistently lower than they had been a decade earlier. Between 1865–9 and 1875–9, Bedfordshire, Buckinghamshire, Hertfordshire and Huntingdonshire recorded falls in excess of thirty per cent with only three counties witnessing any increases: Oxford (four per cent), Norfolk (one per cent) and Hampshire (half per cent).

The decline of poaching toward the end of the nineteenth century is generally attributed to economic, cultural and demographic change. Our local data did not see this decline since Game Las cases increased year on year from a low in 1871 through to 1911.

What does the gaol database show for the other categories?

Night Poaching

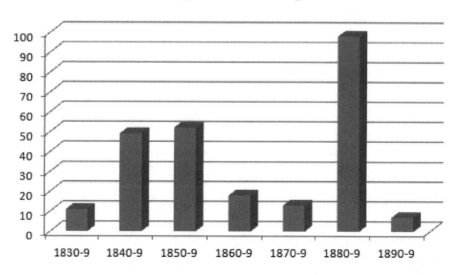

The peak for this crime was the 1880 decade when there were 98 imprisonments. The lower number of cases shows that daytime poaching was by far the most dominant factor and accounted for 90% of all cases.

The other classification is Trespass and this has another 322 records. Again the peak is in the 1850 decade.

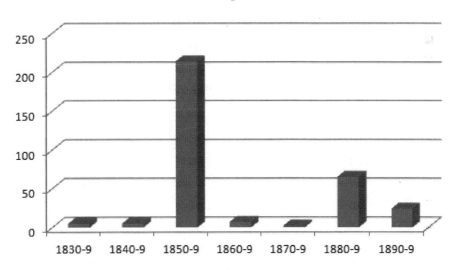

Trespass

There are a very small number of additional records in the 1890s which are indexed by a category 'snaring game'.

Interestingly when searching the records specifically for those prisoners who have had their photograph taken, there were none who have been sentenced under 'Game Law' or 'Night Poaching' offences. Even our earlier reference to the photograph of Jesse Green was due to his Trespass offence at Thurleigh in 1865 rather than his multitude of 'Game Law' convictions.

The total number of Game Law/ Night Poaching/Trespass records for the period 1830 -1898 is 3189 which is 8% of the total number of records in the gaol database.

The 1828 Act on Night Poaching is still active today and made the headlines in 2007. The two men caught taking rabbits and trespassing could have been deported overseas for seven years had an old English poaching law been upheld.

Hereford Magistrates instead fined Mark Adams and Andrew Butts, both from Bargoed, Caerphilly, £385 each after they admitted the offences in August. Under the 1828 Poaching by Night Act, the two men could also have been sentenced to three months hard labour.

The court heard they had been shooting the rabbits to feed to their pet hawks.

Hereford magistrates were told how Adams, 44, and 37-year-old Butts were stopped by police at 0400 GMT on 19 August with 19 rabbits. Three of the animals had been shot on the land at Hoarwithy near Ross-on-Wye belonging to a farmer called Mr Williams. After the police woke him up, Mr Williams said he did not know either of the men and had not given them permission to shoot on his land.

In their defence, the court was told the men had been shooting on the land with a friend a few weeks before who did have permission and had assumed it would be fine. They shot rabbits regularly to either eat themselves or feed to their four birds of prey - two sparrow hawks and two red-tailed hawks. Some of the rabbits they caught were also exchanged with a farmer in Wales for dead chicks which they also fed to their birds.

Adams and Butts told the court they had apologised to Mr Williams for being on his land and for the police waking him up at 0400 in the morning. They admitted trespassing and taking three rabbits without the landowner's permission.

Under the 1828 law, they could have faced three months in jail or three months hard labour until they had paid any money owed to the courts. If they did not pay they could have been "transported beyond seas for seven years or be kept to hard labour in the common gaol for two years". In recent years the law was amended to advise magistrates to impose a fine instead.

Adams and Butts were both fined £45 for taking the rabbits, £225 for trespassing and were ordered to pay the court £115 in costs. It looks as if fines have certainly increased since Victorian times but an inflation calculator shows £5 in 1901 is equivalent to £400 pounds in 2007 hence the fine imposed was almost exactly the same value as we saw in our study period !

The apparent decline of poaching toward the end of the nineteenth century, for example, is generally attributed to economic, cultural and demographic change.

Did the poaching occur seasonally? Looking at cases throughout 1851 we see the following distribution:

Game Law cases throughout the year

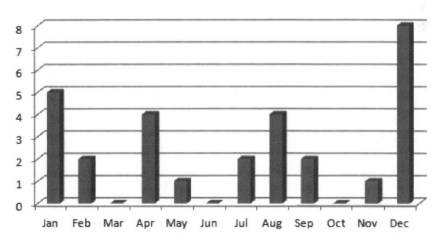

The data supports the earlier findings that most cases occur in the winter months.

The gaol database shows the peak in imprisonments in 1849

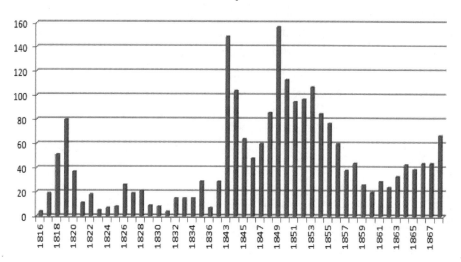

The records show that most poachers are in their early 20s but that the habit can continue into old age.

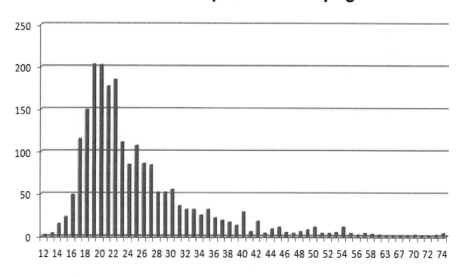

The gaol database records are very poor at recording the occupation of the prisoner. In the 2191 records up to 1868 some 1689 were blank however of the remaining 501, 457 (91%) were labourers and only 44 were other trades of which bricklayers were the most numerous with 6. The records did not qualify the labourer role as Agricultural or industrial. So it's unfortunately impossible to correlate the decline in aglab numbers from 141 in 1871 to only 36 in 1881 with any changes in levels of poaching. We know that 54% of the aglabs were still in the village but only 20% of them were still doing that job.

Can we see ant pattern of poaching in any specific village across North Bedfordshire?

Game Law Imprisonments by Village

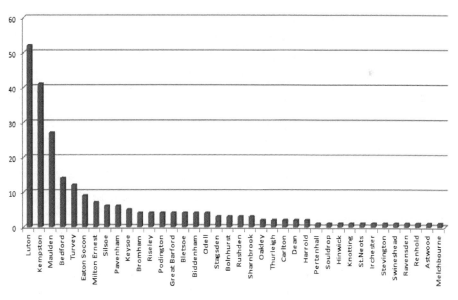

Again the gaol database records are weak in this area. 1300 of the 2191 records up to 1868 were blank. Filtering out all villages except those near to Sharnbrook gives a distribution showing how low the numbers are relative to urban areas such as Luton, Kempston and Bedford. It's obviously not true that it is purely a pastime for agricultural labourers.

It is however very true that pride in poaching skills was a feature of the countryside. This is reflected in the work of HE Bates where he wrote about several people who were identifiable to the locals. One such man was his **Great Uncle Joseph Betts**, whose likeness was interwoven with Uncle Silas in a series of stories, and Sam Smith who had been a chum with whom he had learnt a little about poaching as they had walked the countryside together, and was the basis for the book 'The Poacher'.

A recent photograph in the Stodden Hundred website showed that amongst country folk this pride is still abundant. The picture from 2004 shows Mr and Mrs Fred Squirrel from Wellingborough Row, Upper Dean. They both worked as boot and shoe repairers in a workshop attached to the house. The report goes out of its way to state that Fred was a highly-skilled poacher whilst his wife was well skilled in making medicines from local plants.

References:

(1) The gamekeeper's directory: containing instructions for the preservation of game, destruction of vermin and the prevention of poaching etc Thomas Burgeland Johnson, 1851

(2) Rural and Urban Poaching in Victorian England H Osborne, M Winstanley, Rural History (2006) 17,2 187-212

Chapter Thirteen: Stealing Boots and Shoes

We have seen how theft is habitually one of the most common crimes. The courts have always dealt heavily with the theft of money and valuables such as jewellery and watches. Within the countryside many thefts relate to agricultural products e.g. Robert Toll had a very severe sentence at the

Prisoner record from Bedford

Offence details

Name: Robert Toll

Age: 64

Date of Offence: 26th September 1863

Offence: Stealing barley the property of one John Fobee at Steventon on the 21st Feb. 1863.

Sentence: 10 Years Penal Servitude

Type of trial: Bedfordshire Quarter Sessions

Quarter Sessions of 10 year Penal Servitude for stealing Barley at Stevington. He had had 5 previous convictions for theft of such things as Mangol wurzels, apple trees, sacks and clothes. This sentence seems harsh when you find that the very next record in the database is for William Craddock who with Robert

Jordan did wilfully murder Frederick Budd. For that crime they were both sentenced to the lesser sentence of 7 years penal servitude.

The courts were particularly harsh on thefts of items that the victim used in their occupation e.g. agricultural tools. The removal of the means of the victim to earn money was serious and sentences were lengthy.

Most thefts in the cases heard at the Summary courts were opportunistic thefts. Whilst browsing through the charges and the witness statement it was interesting to see how many cases related to the theft of boots or shoes.

The total number of records in the gaol database between 1830 -1899 is over 41,000. The distribution shows the highest number in the 1850s.

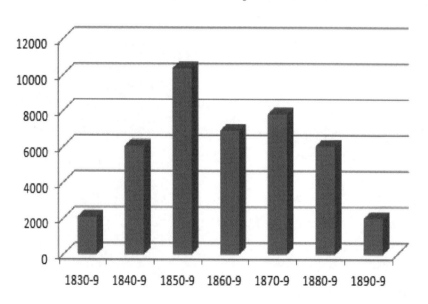

Gaol records by decade

A search of the database for the word 'steal' shows 11,235 records and the distribution again shows the peak in the 1850 decade.

Gaol records for STEALING by decade

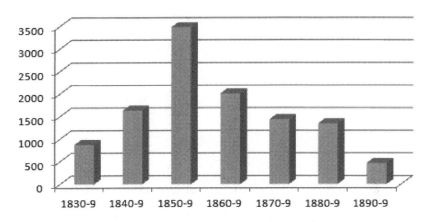

The more specific search for 'stealing boots', shows an almost exponential increase in the number of records across the decades. There were 148 records relating to this crime between 1830 and 1899.

Gaol records for Stealing Boots

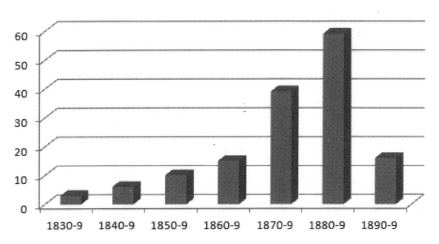

If you add records relating to the 'stealing shoes' there is still an increase but less marked.

Gaol records for stealing boots and/or shoes by decade

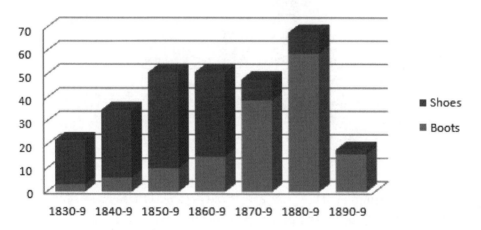

The number of records in the individual study years was quite low with the peak occurring in 1881.

Gaol records for stealing boots

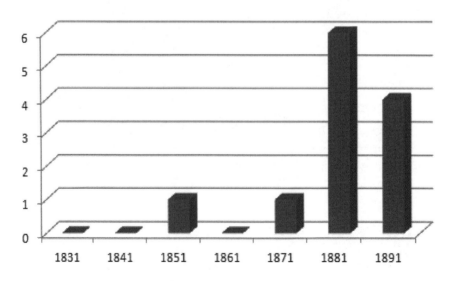

	First Name	Last Name	Age	Committal Year	Residence(town/village)	Birth Town	Offence	Sentence	Document Ref
Detail	Charles	Wood	21	1830	Northampton		Stealing Boots		BLARS QGV10/1
Detail	Thomas	Langridge	30	1836	Luton		Stealing Boots	6 Calendar Months	BLARS QGV10/1
Detail	William	Fisher	23	1837	Stotfold	Stotfold	Stealing Boots	6 Weeks Hard Labour	BLARS QGV10/2
Detail	John	Chesham	18	1844			Stealing Boots	1 Calendar Month Hard Labour	BLARS QGV10/2
Detail	Ellen	Rush	17	1845	Dunstable	Woburn	Stealing boots	6 Weeks Hard Labour 1 week Solitary	BLARS QGV10/2
Detail	James	Fitch	31	1846		Nottingham	Stealing Boots	1 Calendar Month Hard Labour	BLARS QGV10/2
Detail	Julia	Cains	21	1846		Westminster	Stealing Boots	3 Calendar Months Hard Labour	BLARS QGV10/2
Detail	Elizabeth	Smith	28	1846		Derby	Stealing Boots		BLARS QGV10/2
Detail	Anna	Stokes	26	1848		Bristol	Stealing Boots	2 Calendar Months	BLARS QGV10/2
Detail	Eli	Smith	21	1851			Stealing boots etc.	Acquitted	BLARS QGV12/1
Detail	Martin	Walsh	20	1852			Stealing boots	7 [years]	BLARS QGV13/1
Detail	Sarah	Burr	0	1853			Stealing boots	Acquitted	BLARS QGV12/1
Detail	Winifred	Young	30	1854			Stealing Boots	6 Weeks Hard Labour H.C.	BLARS QGV12/1
Detail	Charles	Maynard	21	1854	London	Taunton	Stealing Boots		BLARS QGV10/3
Detail	William	Henshaw	16	1857			Stealing Boots [Borough]	14 Days Hard Labour	BLARS QGV12/1
Detail	Thomas	Birchnall	16	1857			Stealing boots. [Borough]	14 Days Hard Labour	BLARS QGV12/1
Detail	Henry	McDonald	32	1857			Stealing Boot Tops etc (borough)	4 Calendar Months Hard Labour	BLARS QGV12/1
Detail	Hannah	Hammond	27	1858			Stealing Boots	14 Days Hard Labour	BLARS QGV12/1
Detail	James Frederick	Williams	38	1859			Stealing Boots	6 Weeks Hard Labour	BLARS QGV12/1
Detail	Ann	Harris	36	1862			Stealing boots, Fowl Stealing	6 Weeks Hard Labour	BLARS QGV12/1
Detail	Louisa	Badcock	30	1862			Fowl stealing. Stealing Boots	6 Weeks Hard Labour	BLARS QGV12/1
Detail	Ann	Varney	22	1862			Stealing boots	1 Calendar Month Hard Labour	BLARS QGV12/1
Detail	George	Pearson	20	1862			Stealing boots	3 Calendar Months Hard Labour	BLARS QGV12/1
Detail	William	Warren	34	1863			Stealing Boots	14 Days Hard Labour	BLARS QGV12/1
Detail	Edward	Lansbury	16	1865			Stealing Boots	8 Calendar Months Hard Labour	BLARS QGV12/1

The listing of the earlier records in the database show 2 acquittals, and many sentences of a period between 1 and 3 months. There were two cases which saw much harsher sentences; one in 1865 at the Assizes for 8 months hard labour for Edward Lansbury , aged 16. He had one previous conviction but it is not detailed. The record does show he had spent 3 years in the Reformatory School and that he was discharged from gaol after the 8 months.   The second harsh sentence was given to Martin Walsh, aged 20, who was actually sentenced by the Warwick Quarter Sessions in 1852 to 7 years. He had two previous convictions for theft in Hertfordshire and had served sentences of 3 months hard labour and 9 months hard labour. The particular imprisonment at Bedford was disposed by sending him to the "Defence" Hulk, Woolwich.

The sentence could have been even harsher if the same crime had been committed earlier in the century. William Haynes, aged 44 from Cople, was sentenced to 7 years transportation in the Michaelmas 1818 sessions. After two months in Bedford Gaol he was sent to the "Justitia" Hulk at Woolwich.

From there he was one of 131 convicts who sailed on the 393 ton ship "Canada" from London on the 23rd April 1819. The Captain was Alexander Spain and he arrived in New South Wales on 1st September.

Joseph Wright's sentence of 2 months hard labour also seems harsh when you see that he only stole one boot. This theft in Bedford Borough in 1865 was his second offence; would he have received a longer sentence if he took the pair?

Of the 148 records relating to Stealing Boots some 10% received a sentence of 14 days hard labour which was the sentenced most often issued.

Thefts of Boots per year

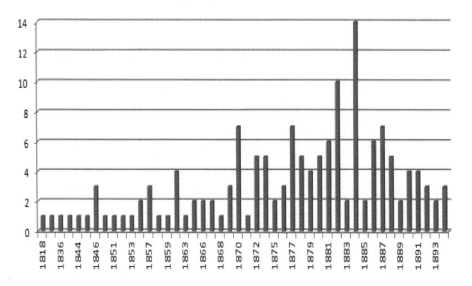

The peak of thefts of boots according to the gaol database was seen in 1884.

Maybe it was the closeness of the shoe industry in Northamptonshire that made boots and shoes a target. The shoe industry in nearby Rushden was however still in its infancy in 1880s since there were only ca. 17 firms compared to the peak of 106 in 1920.

Our earlier research on policing in North Bedfordshire highlighted the importance of boots to the police. There were many examples where the medical status of the policeman deteriorated after many years of walking long rural beats. The importance of good quality boots was eventually recognised by the concession of a regular payment to cover the cost of the constable's boots.

Of course, boots and shoes were not the only targets when thieves stole items of clothing. Even more popular that boots were coats; the theft of a coat or coats accounts for over 200 records between 1830 and 1899. The theft of shirts was less common but still accounted for 125 records in that same period.

Were there any thefts of boots seen in the Sharnbrook petty session records? The simple answer is NO; there was one case in 1891 where Thomas Wright was found guilty of stealing an overcoat, value 2s. Thomas was only aged 10 hence was not imprisoned but was given 13 days to pay a fine of £1 plus was whipped with 6 strokes of the birch.

A young waif steals a pair of boots

The repeated theft of clothing could lead to a very harsh sentence. George Williams, aka John Smith or James Varnes, was convicted at the Bedford Quarter Sessions in 1866 of stealing a coat, cord trousers and other articles value 8s and was sentenced to 7 years penal servitude. George, aged 26, a carpenter born in Long DItton, Surrey had two previous convictions for stealing clothing in 1863.

Prisoner record from Bedford

Offence details

Name: George Williams

Age: 26

Date of Offence: 9th December 1865

Offence: Stealing one black coat, one pair of cord trousers, and other articles together of the value of 8 shillings.

Sentence: 7 Years Penal Servitude

Type of trial: Bedfordshire Quarter Sessions

Samuel Clark and James Westley, two young navvies of Wymington, were charged at Wellingborough court in 1883 with stealing two pairs of cricket shoes, three cricket balls, and five lawn tennis balls, value 20s., the boots the property of Messrs. John and W. Claridge, and the other articles the property of the Rushden Cricket Club.—Charles Bull, the tent manager of the club, deposed that he found the box had been broken into and the above named articles stolen. He identified the articles produced. Abel Young and Samuel Mitchell, lads of Wymington, deposed that they each had bought a cricket ball from Smith for which they gave him sixpence. The former witness said that after he bought the ball Smith told him he had taken it from the Rushden cricket ground. PS Webster said that on Monday from what Smith told him he went to Young, who gave him a cricket ball and a tennis ball which he said he had bought of Smith. He then charged Smith, who said that he and Jimmy Westley broke open the window about 10 o'clock and took the balls between them; they each took a pair of boots, and concealed them in the hedge until evening, when they threw them into a pond at Wymington. On the way to Wellingborough, the sergeant met Westley and charged him with being an accomplice, when Westley admitted taking the balls, but said he knew nothing of the boots. Westley made a statement that they did not take any boots when they stole the balls. Charles Bull recalled, said there might have been other balls in the tent. The boy Young was also questioned by the Chairman as to the date he bought the ball, and he still said he purchased them on the 16th. Some conversation arose and from further statements it appeared that prisoners had been to the tent twice. Prisoners pleaded guilty and were sent to prison for three weeks.

One of the last cases we shall mention is that of Thomas Bates who in 1881 was also convicted of stealing a shirt together with 15 pairs of socks at Wymington. Perhaps he knew that this was to be the peak year in the theft of boots! He elected to be tried summarily, pleaded guilty, and was sentenced 1 month hard labour.

So we have looked at different types of crime and the Bedford Gaol database has been invaluable however the limits of the database and the 100 year embargo on personal data sources have certainly curtailed the study. A cursory look at the 1901 records showed an unusual situation in the

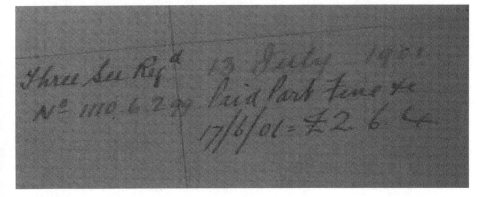

conviction for James Orpin who we have seen earlier. He had been sentenced to a Fine of £2 plus 12s 6d costs or 1 month Hard Labour. The Gaol Register shows that virtually the entire fine was paid within 3 days however because it was a few shillings short he was obliged to stay in gaol and hence he was not discharged until after a full month.

Index